I0474939

The HR Manager's Guide to Immigration Law

James A. Bach
Attorney at Law

Table of Content

Introduction

Foreign workers are a vast resource that American companies can tap to increase productivity and profits. That is especially true in the case of professionals such as engineers and scientists, whose education at foreign and U.S. universities is easily applied to U.S. operations, and whose talent, knowledge, and work ethic may contribute significantly to your company's bottom line. Also, immigrant employees are familiar with the language and customs of other countries, and can help expand markets abroad, coordinate the operations of subsidiaries, and streamline the integration of foreign production facilities and sales offices.

Albert Einstein, Ming Pei, and John Muir, and are just part of a long list of immigrants to the U.S. who have significantly contributed to the science and business of the United States, and who have helped increase the profitability of U.S. companies. Employment-based immigration enables U.S. employers to hire the best and the brightest in a worldwide talent pool of 6 billion people.

Most immigrants buy into the American Dream wholeheartedly, and work very hard to absorb American culture and values. Foreign workers often work harder, smarter, and longer than their American counterparts. The children of legal immigrants are usually exemplary Americans who love the United States, contribute to its advance, and become as American as your own children in this great melting pot. The result is a win-win-win scenario for the employer, the immigrant, and our wonderful country.

There are two broad categories of visas that concern human resources professionals. The first is the "nonimmigrant" working visa that enables the foreign national to work in the

U.S. for a temporary period. Nonimmigrant visas usually can be obtained relatively quickly, and are usually specific to the employer (that is, the status ends when the employment ends). I will devote the most time to the most common and useful working visa, the H-1B visa, but will also provide a summary of the other types of employment-based visas that you should consider.

The second type of visa is the "immigrant" visa (also called "permanent residence status", "lawful permanent residence [LPR] status" and "green card"). The green card provides a permanent right to live and work in the U.S. and often takes many years to obtain. Most employment-based green cards start with a "labor certification," a determination that there is a shortage of U.S. workers for the job. There may be ways to avoid labor certification for special immigrants, such as the world's best athletes and scientists.

This book is designed to be an easy-to-read summary of thousands of pages of government memos, regulations, administrative and court decisions, and statutes. Its purpose is to provide human resources professionals with a working knowledge of the means to hire and employ the best workers in the world. It is not intended to be a scholarly treatise, but a blueprint for a plan of action, a summary of what is feasible and what is not, and a guide for making it happen. We will explore the various types of employment-based visas, and the requirements for each. You will also learn how to work with and evaluate immigration attorneys to achieve results without spending too much money or wasting too much time. Finally, we will explore ways to avoid liability when dealing with foreign workers and those you suspect may not be authorized to work.

Working Visas for Professionals – H-1B

Introduction

H-1B visas are the most popular and useful type of employer-sponsored work visa. They enable "professionals" (usually "white collar" workers with college degrees) to work in the U.S. for six years or more. Preparing and filing an H-1B petition for a new employee can be done quickly, and often the new employee can go onto the payroll in just a few weeks.

There are two basic requirements for H-1B eligibility. First, the worker must have a Bachelor's degree in a specialty field (*or equivalent training and experience*). Second, the job normally must require that degree. Most H-1B workers are engineers, IT workers, scientists, and teachers, but anyone with a Bachelor's degree, or equivalent education and experience, may be eligible for H-1B status. H-1B visas have been granted to a wide range of professionals, including accountants, medical technologists, chemists, database administrators, business managers, statisticians, nurses, and marketing professionals.

In addition to these basic eligibility requirements, there are several employer obligations and liabilities that Congress has added over the years in response to political concerns. These additional employer obligations may seem daunting at first, but usually can be fulfilled with a minimum of time, effort and expense. It is important that the HR manager understands the extent of the employer's obligations in an H-1B case, and closely follows the instructions of the immigration attorney in complying with them. Failure to comply with the regulations can lead to penalties, including payment of back wages to H-1B employees who were underpaid.

Overview of the H-1B petition procedure

The H-1B petition can be prepared as soon as the prospective employee has accepted a job offer. The process essentially involves five steps, as follows:

1. Prepare a "Labor Condition Application" (LCA).[1]
2. Post LCA legal notices at the location where the employee will work.
3. File the LCA with the U.S. Department of Labor (DOL).
4. Comply with LCA requirements, designed to make sure that the foreign employee is paid a salary that is comparable to that of a U.S. worker doing the same job.
5. Submit the H-1B petition to the U.S. Citizenship and Immigration Services (USCIS). This submission will normally consist of the approved LCA, petition forms, a supporting letter, documents that reflect the employee's educational background, and documents that describe the nature of the employer and its ability to hire the employee.

The LCA must be certified by the DOL before the H-1B petition can be filed with the USCIS. Until recently that certification process was instantaneous, but 2009 modifications to the LCA online registration system have resulted in delays of several days or even weeks.

---

[1] Not to be confused with a "Labor Certification Application", used to obtain a green card.

Starting Employment

A law passed in 2000, "AC21"[2], provides that a prospective employee *who is already in H-1B status* with another employer is authorized to work as soon as the H-1B petition is filed with the USCIS. That authorization continues until the H-1B petition is approved or denied. According to the 2011 I-9 Handbook, completing the I-9 for those with this interim work authorization involves writing "AC21" on the I-9 and reviewing the employee's previous H-1B approval notice. The I-9 should then be updated when the H-1B petition is finally approved.

For those who are not already in H-1B status, "Premium Processing" (i.e., expedited processing) of the H-1B petition is possible, by paying an additional filing fee of $1,225. It is certainly annoying to pay an additional fee to motivate the government do what it should do anyway (process the petition in a reasonable amount of time), but Premium Processing often is the only way to get a new H-1B employee onto the payroll quickly. Premium Processing is a money-back guarantee by the USCIS that the petition will be adjudicated within 15 days, although normally the actual processing time is a week or so. A Premium Processing case can be delayed beyond 15 days (with no refund of the $1,225 fee) if the USCIS requests additional documents (which it does in a large number of cases).

The H-1B Quota

In addition to the DOL and USCIS processing time, the H-1B quota is a potential delay factor. Currently the law allows for 85,000 new H-1B visas each year (with 20,000 of those reserved for employees with U.S. Master's degrees). The visas are allocated on a first-come, first-served basis, and by lottery. Typically, a filing period is opened up during the first week in April, and then a lottery is applied if the number

---

[2] American Competitiveness in the Twenty-first Century Act of 2000.

of petitions received during that week exceeds the quota. For most of the past decade, the number of H-1B petitions exceeded the quota. For example, in 2007 and 2008 more than 100,000 petitions were filed during the first week of April. However, in the recession years of 2009, 2010, and 2011, less than 40,000 petitions were received in April.

Some H-1B applicants are not subject to the annual quota, including those who:

1. Are already in H-1B status.
2. Have been in H-1B status within the past 6 years.
3. Will be employed by a college or university.
4. Will be employed by a nonprofit entity (including hospitals) associated with a college or university.
5. Will be employed by a nonprofit or governmental research organization.

H-1B petitions subject to the quota are effective on the following October 1, the start of the government's fiscal year. This 6-month delay, from filing in April to the start of work authorization in October, can present some planning challenges for HR and the hiring managers. Potential H-1B employees who are not already in H-1B status (such as those living outside of the U.S. or in the U.S. in another nonimmigrant status) must be identified, recruited and hired well in advance of their starting date. F-1 students with Practical Training, however, are an exception. If their H-1B petition is accepted for filing under the quota, their Practical Training status is automatically extended to October 1, as long as the H-1B petition is filed before the Practical Training expires. In that case, they can get another I-20 from their college that indicates the automatic extension for I-9 verification.

H-1B Costs

There are four different costs associated with the H-1B process: 1) the USCIS filing fees, 2) the legal fee, 3) administrative resources (including the HR manager's own time), and 4) (rarely) expert witness fees (to evaluate education and experience). All of those costs should be considered together in analyzing and controlling the costs of hiring a foreign national.

The USCIS filing fees are fixed, so there is limited ability to affect that cost. Those fees include a basic filing fee ($325), a "training" fee ($1,500 for employers with more than 25 employees, and $750 for smaller employers), and a "fraud" fee ($500). The training fee is used to train U.S. workers, and the fraud fee is used, among other things, to investigate H-1B violations. The training fee must be paid by the sponsoring employer, and cannot be passed on to the H-1B employee.

Another potential filing fee is the "Premium Processing" fee, the $1,225 charge for processing the petition within 15 days as discussed above. Without Premium Processing, the processing time for an H-1B petition is typically 2 to 5 months. The Premium Processing fee is discretionary, and therefore a place where money can be saved in filing fees. Often it is not required because the employment can begin as soon as the H-1B petition is filed (based on AC21), but the employee or even the attorney may lobby for payment of this fee. It is therefore important to determine whether there is a good reason (worth at least $1,225) for Premium Processing before incurring that expense.

In 2010, Congress imposed an additional filing fee of $2,000 for each H-1B case if the employer has more than 50 employees in the U.S., and more than 50% of its workforce is in H-1B status. This provision[3] was primarily directed to Indian consulting companies, and does not affect most U.S. employers.

The second cost, less fixed, but immediately quantifiable, is the legal fee. Most attorneys charge a flat fee between $1,000 and $3,000 to handle a routine H-1B case (for example, a petition for a software engineer with a college degree in the field), depending on experience, the number of cases, and local market conditions. However, many cases require extra time and skill, and in those cases the fee may be significantly higher. Typical cases that involve greater difficulties (and therefore a higher fee than the fee in a routine case) may include:

    a)   An employee who will work at more than one work site, such as a traveling consultant.

    b)   An executive or key employee who may require additional legal advice and personal attention.

    c)   An employee who does not have a college degree in the field, but who has relevant experience instead.

    d)   A job that the USCIS may not consider a "professional" occupation (such as hotel managers, translators, web designers, and marketing professionals).

    e)   A small startup company that has few employees, does not have a substantial physical presence (such as regular office space), or has been operating at a loss.

    f)   A company that is primarily or solely owned by the H-1B employee.

---

[3] In the *Emergency Supplemental Appropriation for Border Security Act of 2010*.

Many cases involve quite a bit of work to document a potential employee's professional background or the need for a professional. That documentation may include professional evaluations of the employee's diplomas and transcripts, expert opinions from professors and other experts, USCIS decisions in similar cases, letters from former employers, and other proof of prior professional experience.

A third potential cost therefore is the cost of expert opinions from credential evaluators, professors or other industry experts. Those opinions are normally of three types. The first type evaluates a foreign college degree to determine its equivalency to a degree at an accredited university in the U.S. Typically, those evaluations cost under $100. A second type of expert opinion involves the evaluation of the training and experience of an employee who does not have the appropriate college degree, and compares that training and experience to the coursework involved in getting the appropriate degree. Those evaluations may cost $500 or so. Finally, it is often helpful to hire professors or other industry experts to write opinion letters that conclude that a job normally requires a college degree. Those opinions may cost $500 to $2,500.

The final item of cost is administrative time -- the time and resources of the HR professional, hiring manager, and others within the employer's organization. This cost is directly related to the ability and effectiveness of the attorney, and the normal efficiency of the HR department. Effective immigration counsel should be able to keep this administrative time and cost to a minimum (perhaps a half hour per case) in routine H-1B cases, although the extraordinary cases listed above may involve many hours of administrative time.

The Labor Condition Application (LCA)

Before the H-1B petition can be filed, a Labor Condition Application (LCA) must be approved by the Department of Labor. On its surface the LCA process appears to be simple, and in most cases it will be. However, because of the various political compromises made in their formation, the LCA rules are complex and convoluted, and hide pitfalls for the unwary. Fines, back wages, battles with the Department of Labor, and possible exclusion from the H-1B program await employers who do not abide by these Byzantine rules.

Some of the highlights of the LCA rules are as follows:

a) You cannot require the employee to pay the USCIS "training" fee.

The $1,500 CIS training fee ($750 if less than 26 employees) must be paid directly by the employer. The employer <u>cannot seek reimbursement</u> from the employee either directly or indirectly for that portion of the fee.

b) By signing the labor condition application (LCA), the employer is attesting to the following:

1. *For the entire period of authorized employment*, the employer will pay the H-1B employee at least:

   A. the **actual** wage (the amount paid by the employer to other individuals with similar experience and qualifications for the specific position); **and**

   B. the **prevailing** wage (the weighted average salary for that specific occupational classification paid by all employers in the geographic area of intended employment).

The employer must pay the higher of these two numbers (called the "required wage".)

2. The employment of the H-1B alien will not adversely affect the working conditions of workers similarly employed in the area of intended employment.

3. On the date the LCA is signed and submitted, there was no a strike, lockout, or work stoppage related to a labor dispute in the relevant occupation at the place of employment.

4. On or before the date of the LCA, notice of the application was 1) was posted in two conspicuous places at the location(s) of employment, 2) posted electronically on a company intranet, or 3) a collective bargaining representative was notified. The first option is used most of the time.

c) **The employer must pay the higher of the "prevailing wage" and "actual wage" (the "required wage") during the <u>entire</u> period of employment.**

The only exception is if the employee *voluntarily* stops working for a period of time for a reason not related to the employment. For example, if the employee wants to stop working temporarily for vacation, illness, injury, or maternity leave, the employer can stop paying the required wage. It is a good idea to memorialize the employee's request in an email or signed document, and add that memo to the LCA file. However, if the employee is "benched" because there is not enough work available, the wage must still be paid until the employment is terminated. If there is a reduction in salary for any reason (including a transfer from full-time to part-time employment) a new LCA must be submitted.

The obligation to pay the salary stated on the LCA and H-1B petition begins 30 days after the employee is first admitted into the U.S. in H-1B status, or, if the employer is already in the U.S., 60 days after the H-1B petition is approved. **The obligation to pay the salary continues until** the authorized H-1B period expires or **the employer withdraws the petition by notifying the USCIS.**

The required wage must be paid to a salaried H-1B employee at least biweekly, and to an hourly employee at least monthly. There should be no deductions from wages other than taxes and normal benefits for the employee's benefit (such as 401(k) payments). *H-1B expenses cannot be deducted from the paycheck.*

d) **The employer must post the two LCA notices <u>before</u> signing the LCA.**

The LCA notices must be posted for ten calendar days in two conspicuous locations in your offices. The regulations provide the following guidance as to where they must be posted:

> *The notice shall be clearly visible and unobstructed while posted and shall be posted in conspicuous places, where the employer's U.S. workers can readily read the posted notice on their way to or from their place of employment. Appropriate locations for posting notices of the job opportunity include, but are not limited to, locations in the immediate vicinity of the wage and hour notices required by 20 CFR 516.4 or occupational safety and health notices required by 20 CFR 1903.2(a).*

The notices can also be sent to all other employees in the same occupation by e-mail, or posted on the company intranet. *If the employee will work at a client site, notice must be given by posting the notice at the client site, or by providing notice by email or intranet to the employees in your company <u>and the client's company</u>.* That is one reason why it can be logistically difficult to place H-1B employees at client sites for long periods of time.

e) **When the employment ends, the employer must withdraw the LCA and notify the USCIS.**

The obligation to pay the salary promised in the H-1B documents continues until there has been a *bona fide termination* of the employment relationship. (See discussion in Chapter 12).

The attorney can assist in making sure that an employee is properly terminated so the salary obligation is ended. **Employers who do not properly terminate the H-1B status may be liable for the employee's full salary for several years, even if the employee has found other employment.**

f) **The employer must prepare and retain an "Actual Wage Memorandum."**

The "Actual Wage Memorandum" must state the wage to be paid to the H-IB employee, and describe how it is consistent with the wages paid to other employees of the company who have similar backgrounds and jobs. The regulations require a showing of "how the wage paid [to the H-1B employee] relates to all other [employees] with similar experience and qualifications for the specific employment in question." The Actual Wage Memorandum must be detailed enough to enable a third party to "understand how the employer applied its pay system to arrive at the actual wage for its H-1B nonimmigrant(s)."

The Actual Wage Memorandum must state the business-related factors that are used in setting wages and the manner in which they are implemented (for example, the wage/salary range for the position and the pay differentials for various factors such as education, job experience, job duties and demonstrated past performance). Finally, the Actual Wage Memorandum must explain that the benefits provided to the H-1B employee are consistent with the benefits provided to other employees.

g) **The employer must maintain an "LCA file" for the entire time the employee is in H-1B status, plus one year.**

The contents of the LCA file will include:

1) The signed original LCA.
2) The prevailing wage document (either a salary survey or a salary determination from the state job office).
3) The two LCA notices (with a notation as to the locations and dates of posting).
4) The Actual Wage Memorandum.

h) **The employee cannot pay the attorney's fee or other costs related to the H-1B if paying those fees and costs would cause the employee's net wage to dip below the higher of 1) the "actual wage" or 2) the "prevailing wage."**

For example, if the "prevailing wage" is $75,000, the employee earns $77,000 (in this example, also the "actual wage"), and the H-1B legal fee is $3,000, by paying the legal fee the employee's net salary would be $74,000, an amount below the "prevailing wage".

i) **The Department of Labor may find a violation if the employee pays *any* of the H-1B legal fees and costs.**

The regulations do not expressly prohibit the employee from paying the legal fees and costs, with the sole exception of the training fee. However, the Department of Labor (DOL) may not agree, and it has not provided specific guidance. The most conservative approach (to avoid all possibility of incurring fines or other penalties for this reason) is for the employer to pay all H-1B legal fees and costs.

j) **The LCA and H-1B petition must be amended if there is a material change in the employment.**

Material changes in employment requiring amendment include any change in the location of the employment, reduction of the salary below the amount stated on the H-1B petition, and significant changes in job duties.

Short-Term Placements

In general, an H-1B employee cannot work at a new location (one not designated on the LCA) for more than 30 days in a one-year period, unless an LCA is filed and LCA notices are posted at that location <u>before</u> the employee begins work at that location.

This rule presents a challenge for employers who wish to place the employee at client sites for consulting assignments (common in the IT field). Each long-term assignment (of 30 days or more) requires an LCA for the assigned work location (including posting of the LCA notices at that location).

Many if not most IT companies who hire H-1B employees to work as consultants at client sites violate this requirement, because they do not want to ask their clients to post LCA notices at the work site, or because they are simply unaware of the requirement. However, it is important to keep in mind that the LCA and H-1B petition are specific to the location, and if the location changes new filings are required.

For assignments of less than 30 days, an LCA is not required, but the employer must pay the travel expenses (including the actual cost of lodging, transportation, meals and "miscellaneous expenses") for both work days and non-workdays.

Also, a new LCA is not required for an assignment of 30 to 60 days if certain guidelines are met. If an office or workstation is maintained for the employee at the central location (for which the LCA was obtained), the 30-day limit on short-term placements is increased to 60 days per year. To be eligible for the extended 60-day short-term placement exception the employee must reside near the office or workstation, and must spend a substantial amount of his or her time there.

The regulations also provide for an LCA exemption for an employee who is "peripatetic", a Greek word that means "walking about" (and a word that you are unlikely to encounter outside of the context of H-1B visas!). A peripatetic worker is someone like a traveling salesperson who is in a job that by its nature requires frequent travel to other locations on a short-term basis. The peripatetic worker can work up to five consecutive days at other work sites, and there is no limit to the total number of days per year that can be spent at the other worksites (as long as each visit is less than six days).

Another exemption is provided for an H-1B employee who spends most of his or her time at a primary worksite (for which an LCA was obtained) but who occasionally visits other sites on a short-term basis. In that case, the employee can visit for up to ten consecutive days, and like the peripatetic worker is not subject to a limit of total days visiting the site each year.

The regulations indicate that these visits to an outside location can be recurring, but they cannot be excessive. For example, an attempt to avoid LCAs by having the employee continually move between two work sites for five days each time, would probably be viewed as a violation of the letter and spirit of the regulations, and could lead to LCA penalties.

Examples in the regulations of peripatetic workers (eligible to stay for five days) and short-term visitors who have a central workplace (eligible to stay for ten days) include a computer engineer who troubleshoots client problems on-site, and an outside auditor conducting reviews at client companies.

For a traveling consultant with longer-term assignments, compliance with the LCA requirements, including posting at each work site, can be onerous or prohibitive. Those compliance requirements should be considering in planning assignments for H-1B employees, and even whether to hire them for that position in the first place.

H-1B Dependent Employees

An employer is "H-1B dependent" if it has more than a prescribed number of H-1B employees, as follows:

Company Size	Number of H-1B Employees
25 employees or less	7
26 to 50 employees	12
More than 50 employees	15% of workforce

However, the additional requirements for "H-1B dependent" employers do not apply to employees who 1) have a Master's degree, *or* 2) will earn at least $60,000 per year. This $60,000 threshold was established more than a decade ago, when $60,000 appeared to be a significant salary for an H-1B professional. Now it is at the low end for most professional positions, and is not much of a barrier. It is therefore unlikely that there will be too many cases where the additional requirements for "H-1B dependent" employers must be fulfilled, and their further complexities are therefore beyond our discussion here.

H-1B Investigations and Penalties

Failure to follow the LCA rules can lead to various penalties including payment of back wages (if the Department of Labor determines that the employer was not paying the required wage), fines, and "debarment" (limitations on filing H-1B and immigrant visa petitions).

Most Department of Labor (DOL) investigations relating to H-1B cases involve a failure to pay the required wage, and most investigations start with a complaint from a disgruntled H-1B employee (who may believe he or she is not paid the required wage).

DOL investigations usually begin with a telephone call to the person named on the LCA. The best approach for dealing with a DOL investigation is to get an attorney involved as soon as possible. It is therefore best not to speak to the investigator immediately, but instead get the investigator's name and telephone number and offer to call him or her back to set up a meeting once a response strategy can be developed with the attorney.

Time Limitation

H-1B visas are usually issued for an initial period of three years, and there is generally a total limit of six year in the U.S. in H-1B status. After leaving the U.S. for at least one year, the employee can return for another six years.

However, this six-year limit does not apply if the employee begins the process of applying for permanent residence status, by filing a labor certification or immigrant visa petition, before the end of the 5th year in H-1B status. In that case, he or she can continue to extend the H-1B status indefinitely until the green card is issued.

H-1B Treaty Substitutes for Nationals of Certain Countries (TN, E-3, and H-1B1)

Treaties with certain trading partners of the U.S. have created visa categories for professionals from those countries that are unavailable to everyone else. For example, the U.S. has a special relationship with Mexico and Canada because they are our close neighbors and huge trading partners, and with Australia because it has supported us in all of our wars, included the unpopular ones. Chile and Singapore are on the list because they were perceived to be potentially important trading partners.

These special visas should always be evaluated as a substitute for H-1B visas because the H-1B quota may be filled, additional filing fees can be avoided, and in some cases the LCA can be avoided.

Eligibility for these special visas depends on *citizenship*, not place of birth.[4] For example a person born in China who subsequently becomes an Australian citizen would be eligible for an E-3 visa.

---

[4] There is a different system of country chargeabilit for the green card quotas, which depend only on place of birth, and not country of citizenship.

TN Status

The most important of these treaties is NAFTA (the North American Free Trade Agreement) which has created a special category for professionals from Canada and Mexico ("TN status"). TN eligibility is limited to those professional workers who are listed in the treaty, as follows:

—Accountant—Baccalaureate or Licenciatura Degree; or C.P.A., C.A., C.G.A., or C.M.A.

—Architect—Baccalaureate or Licenciatura Degree; or state/provincial license.[5]

—Computer Systems Analyst—Baccalaureate or Licenciatura Degree; or Post-Secondary Diploma[6] or Post Secondary Certificate[7] and three years' experience.

—Disaster relief insurance claims adjuster (claims adjuster employed by an insurance company located in the territory of a Party, or an independent claims adjuster)—Baccalaureate or Licenciatura Degree and successful completion of training in the appropriate areas of insurance adjustment pertaining to disaster relief claims; or three years experience in claims adjustment and

---

[5] The terms "state/provincial license" and "state/provincial/federal license" mean any document issued by a state, provincial, or federal government, as the case may be, or under its authority, but not by a local government, that permits a person to engage in a regulated activity or profession.

[6] "Post Secondary Diploma" means a credential issued, on completion of two or more years of post secondary education, by an accredited academic institution in Canada or the United States.

[7] "Post Secondary Certificate" means a certificate issued, on completion of two or more years of post secondary education at an academic institution, by the federal government of Mexico or a state government in Mexico, an academic institution recognized by the federal government or a state government, or an academic institution created by federal or state law.

successful completion of training in the appropriate areas of insurance adjustment pertaining to disaster relief claims.

—Economist—Baccalaureate or Licenciatura Degree.

—Engineer—Baccalaureate or Licenciatura Degree; or state/provincial license.

—Forester—Baccalaureate or Licenciatura Degree; or state/provincial license.

—Graphic Designer—Baccalaureate or Licenciatura Degree; or Post-Secondary Diploma or Post-Secondary Certificate and three years experience.

—Hotel Manager—Baccalaureate or Licenciatura Degree in hotel/restaurant management; or Post-Secondary Diploma or Post Secondary Certificate in hotel/restaurant management and three years experience in hotel/restaurant management.

—Industrial Designer—Baccalaureate or Licenciatura Degree; or Post-Secondary Diploma or Post Secondary Certificate, and three years experience.

—Interior Designer—Baccalaureate or Licenciatura Degree or Post-Secondary Diploma or Post-Secondary Certificate, and three years experience.

—Land Surveyor—Baccalaureate or Licenciatura Degree or state/provincial/federal license.

—Landscape Architect—Baccalaureate or Licenciatura Degree.

—Lawyer (including Notary in the province of Quebec)— L.L.B., J.D., L.L.L., B.C.L., or Licenciatura degree (five years); or membership in a state/provincial bar.

—Librarian—M.L.S., or B.L.S. (for which another Baccalaureate or Licenciatura Degree was a prerequisite).

—Management Consultant—Baccalaureate or Licenciatura Degree; or equivalent professional experience as established by statement or professional credential attesting to five years experience as a management consultant, or five years experience in a field of specialty related to the consulting agreement.

—Mathematician (including Statistician)—Baccalaureate or Licenciatura Degree.[8]

—Range Manager/Range Conservationist—Baccalaureate or Licenciatura Degree.

—Research Assistant (working in a post-secondary educational institution)—Baccalaureate or Licenciatura Degree.

—Scientific Technician/Technologist[9] —Possession of (a) theoretical knowledge of any of the following disciplines: agricultural sciences, astronomy, biology, chemistry, engineering, forestry, geology, geophysics, meteorology, or physics; and (b) the ability to solve practical problems in any of those disciplines, or the ability to apply principles of any of those disciplines to basic or applied research.

—Social Worker—Baccalaureate or Licenciatura Degree.

---

[8] The term "Mathematician" includes the profession of Actuary. An Actuary must satisfy the necessary requirements to be recognized as an actuary by a professional actuarial association or society. A professional actuarial association or society means a professional actuarial association or society operating in the territory of at least one of the Parties.

[9] A business person in this category must be seeking temporary entry for work in direct support of professionals in agricultural sciences, astronomy, biology, chemistry, engineering, forestry, geology, geophysics, meteorology or physics.

—Sylviculturist (including Forestry Specialist)—Baccalaureate or Licenciatura Degree.

—Technical Publications Writer—Baccalaureate or Licenciatura Degree, or Post-Secondary Diploma or Post-Secondary Certificate, and three years experience.

—Urban Planner (including Geographer)—Baccalaureate or Licenciatura Degree.

—Vocational Counselor—Baccalaureate or Licenciatura Degree.

MEDICAL/ALLIED PROFESSIONALS

—Dentist—D.D.S., D.M.D., Doctor en Odontologia or Doctor en Cirugia Dental or state/provincial license.

—Dietitian—Baccalaureate or Licenciatura Degree; or state/provincial license.

—Medical Laboratory Technologist (Canada)/Medical Technologist (Mexico and the United States)[10] — Baccalaureate or Licenciatura Degree; or Post-Secondary Diploma or Post-Secondary Certificate, and three years experience.

—Nutritionist—Baccalaureate or Licenciatura Degree.

—Occupational Therapist—Baccalaureate or Licenciatura Degree; or state/provincial license.

—Pharmacist—Baccalaureate or Licenciatura Degree; or state/provincial license.

---

[10] A business person in this category must be seeking temporary entry to perform in a laboratory chemical, biological, hematological, immunologic, microscopic or bacteriological tests and analyses for diagnosis, treatment, or prevention of diseases.

—Physician (teaching or research only)—M.D. Doctor en Medicina; or state/provincial license.

—Physiotherapist/Physical Therapist—Baccalaureate or Licenciatura Degree; or state/provincial license.

—Psychologist—state/provincial license; or Licenciatura Degree.

—Recreational Therapist-Baccalaureate or Licenciatura Degree.

—Registered nurse—state/provincial license or Licenciatura Degree.

—Veterinarian—D.V.M., D.M.V., or Doctor en Veterinaria; or state/provincial license.

SCIENTIST

—Agriculturist (including Agronomist)—Baccalaureate or Licenciatura Degree.

—Animal Breeder—Baccalaureate or Licenciatura Degree.

—Animal Scientist—Baccalaureate or Licenciatura Degree.

—Apiculturist—Baccalaureate or Licenciatura Degree.

—Astronomer—Baccalaureate or Licenciatura Degree.

—Biochemist—Baccalaureate or Licenciatura Degree.

—Biologist—Baccalaureate or Licenciatura Degree.[11]

—Chemist—Baccalaureate or Licenciatura Degree.

—Dairy Scientist—Baccalaureate or Licenciatura Degree.

—Entomologist—Baccalaureate or Licenciatura Degree.

---

[11] The term "Biologist" includes the profession of Plant Pathologist.

—Epidemiologist—Baccalaureate or Licenciatura Degree.

—Geneticist—Baccalaureate or Licenciatura Degree.

—Geochemist—Baccalaureate or Licenciatura Degree.

—Geologist—Baccalaureate or Licenciatura Degree.

—Geophysicist (including Oceanographer in Mexico and the United States)—Baccalaureate or Licenciatura Degree.

—Horticulturist—Baccalaureate or Licenciatura Degree.

—Meteorologist—Baccalaureate or Licenciatura Degree.

—Pharmacologist—Baccalaureate or Licenciatura Degree.

—Physicist (including Oceanographer in Canada— Baccalaureate or Licenciatura Degree.

—Plant Breeder—Baccalaureate or Licenciatura Degree.

—Poultry Scientist—Baccalaureate or Licenciatura Degree.

—Soil Scientist—Baccalaureate or Licenciatura Degree.

—Zoologist—Baccalaureate or Licenciatura Degree.

TEACHER

—College—Baccalaureate or Licenciatura Degree.

—Seminary—Baccalaureate or Licenciatura Degree.

—University—Baccalaureate or Licenciatura Degree.

If a potential employee is from Canada or Mexico, these TN occupational categories should be analyzed carefully to determine if there is any basis for asserting that the proposed job is included.

The "Management Consultant" category is often used as a catch-all category for those who do not fall into any of the other categories. Despite (or because of) its popularity, applications for TN status for Management Consultants are often denied, so care must be taken in their preparation.

There two primary restrictions on the Management Consultant category that are not apparent in the NAFTA treaty itself. First, the job must be "supernumerary", that is it must be a special consulting role and not a regular position in the company. Second, the job must be temporary, and must end when the objectives of the consulting are accomplished. The following description from the 1999 NAFTA Handbook (INS) still drives policy in this area:

> **"Management consultants** provide services that are directed toward improving the managerial, operating, and economic performance of public and private entities by analyzing and resolving strategic and operating problems and thereby improving the entity's goals, objectives, policies, strategies, administration, organization, and operation. Management consultants are usually independent contractors or employees of consulting firms under contracts to U.S. entities. They may be salaried employees of the U.S. entities to which they are providing services only when they are not assuming existing positions or filling newly created positions. As a salaried employee of such an U.S. entity, they may only fill supernumerary temporary positions."

Another popular TN category is "Computer Systems Analysts", and it may be used to include a variety of computer professionals. The NAFTA Handbook describes this occupation as:

> "an information specialist who analyzes how data processing can be applied to the specific needs of users and who designs and implements computer-based processing systems. Systems analysts study the organization itself to identify its information needs and design computer systems that meet those needs."

This appears to be a fairly broad definition that would include many different types of computer and information professionals. However, in practice many professionals, for example web designers, who may appear to fit in this category may have their TN applications denied. The NAFTA Handbook states that this category does not include "programmers", and other guidance from the government has indicated that software engineers should be included in the "Engineers" category rather than with "Computer Systems Analysts."

The manner of applying for TN status depends on whether the employee is a citizen of Canada or Mexico. Unlike those from other countries, Canadians do not need a visa to enter the United States. That is true regardless of the type of visa status they seek in the U.S. (with the sole exception of E-1 and E-2 visas).

Also, TN status does not normally depend on a visa petition that is first approved by the USCIS (as in the case of H-1B and L-1 status). Accordingly, a Canadian can apply for TN status at a port of entry (an international airport in Canada, or a land border like Buffalo, New York) as soon as she has evidence of a job offer. The ability of Canadians to bypass both the USCIS and the U.S. Embassy or Consulate creates the major advantage of the TN status over other employment categories like H-1B. Conceivably, a TN applicant can obtain the right to work for a new employer within 24 hours of receiving the job offer.

Like the Canadian TN applicant, an applicant from Mexico does not need a pre-approved visa petition, but, unlike the Canadian, does need a visa. The Mexican employee must submit the application for a TN visa to the U.S. Embassy in Mexico City, or one of the U.S. consulates in Mexico (Ciudad Juarez, Tijuana, Merida, Guadalajara, Puerto Vallarta, Nogales, Matamoros, Merida, or Hermosillo). Processing times for issuing the TN visa for Mexicans can range from several days to several weeks.

Like the H-1B status, TN status is normally issued for a period of three years. That is a new development in 2009; previously TN status was granted in increments of one year. There is no legal time limit for TN visas, as there is for H-1B status (six years), but there is a requirement that the employment be "temporary". That may become more difficult to establish after many years, but often those in TN status are often able to extend their TN status for more than a decade.

On its face, obtaining the TN status is easy: the employee must simply submit evidence that he or she 1) has the education and/or experience to qualify for one of the professional categories listed above, and 2) has an offer for temporary employment in that category. In practice, however, many problems can arise, and TN applicants, even those who have previously been in TN status, can be denied entry and get stuck outside of the U.S.

One of the problems can be overly strict or untrained officers. Unlike USCIS examiners whose only function is to adjudicate certain types of applications, the CBP (Customs and Border Protection) officers are also responsible for customs and many other aspects of eligibility to enter the U.S. Although some are designated as "Free Trade Officers" who theoretically have expertise with TN status, often the examiner on duty who will make the decision may not have very much experience. Also, many aspects of TN adjudication are subjective and involve judgment calls that may result in denials.

Another problem can be that employers and employees believe that they have presented an adequate case for TN classification, when in fact there are obstacles to approval that they have not anticipated, or worse, they have created in their application. For example, an employer may attempt to fill a vacant position with a TN employee in the "Management Consultant" category without adequately proving that the job is supernumerary and temporary.

E-3 Visas

E-3 visas are an H-1B substitute that enable professional employment for Australians only, and should be considered every time the prospective employee is Australian. The E-3 visa has the following advantages over the H-1B visa:

1. It is faster. The application for the E-3 visa is submitted directly to the U.S. Consulate, and the weeks or months required for H-1B petition processing by the USCIS can be avoided.
2. It is cheaper. The USCIS filing fees of up to $3,550 are avoided.
3. It is not subject to the H-1B quota. An application can therefore be made at any time during the year, and a lengthy lead time can be avoided.
4. The spouse of an E-3 visa holder can be authorized to work.

As with an H-1B petition, a Labor Condition Application (LCA) is required before submitting the E-3 application. Normally, LCA processing takes a week or two.

Often the expiration dates of the E-3 visa, I-94 (the document that determines the period of authorized stay in the U.S.), and the LCA are different, and must all be tracked so that each can be extended before they expire.

Unlike an H-1B petition, an E-3 petition extension does not automatically extend the right to work while it is pending. It should therefore be filed six months or so before the expiration date to ensure that there is plenty of time for petition processing.

H-1B1 Visas

H-1B1 visas are only available to nationals of Chile or Singapore. Like E-3 visas, they are not subject to the H-1B quota. Instead, they have their own quota (1,400 for Chile and 5,400 for Singapore). So far, the H-1B1 quotas have never been oversubscribed, so an H-1B1 applicant, like an E-3 applicant, can apply for the visa at any time of the year.

Intracompany Transferees (L-1 visas)

CHAPTER

3

Multi-national corporations should consider L-1 visas before all other temporary working visas. Advantages of L-1 status over H-1B status include the following:

1. A Labor Condition Application (LCA) is not required, so the employee does not have to be paid a "prevailing wage".
2. There is no potential liability for LCA violations (for example, back wages and fines for failing to pay a prevailing wage, or for not properly terminating the employee).
3. There is no legal requirement to pay for return transportation.
4. The L-1 employee can work anywhere in the U.S., without the necessity of an LCA for each location.
5. *Spouses of L-1 employees are eligible to work!*

Like the H-1B visa, the L-1 visa begins with a petition to the USCIS. Once the petition is approved, the employee will present the petition approval to a U.S. Consulate or Embassy abroad, and obtain a the L-1 visa (a stamp in the passport that will be used to gain entry into the U.S.).

L-1 Eligibility Requirements

There are L-1 eligibility requirements for both the U.S. employer and the employee. The employer must be either

1. the same company as,
2. a subsidiary of,
3. a parent of, or
4. an affiliate of

the company that has employed the employee for at least one year with in the past three years.

A U.S. parent or subsidiary of the foreign company means that one company owns at least 50% of the other. An "affiliate" means that a third company or person owns and controls both the U.S. and the foreign companies. If several companies or people own both companies, they are "affiliates" only if those companies or people own a total a controlling interest *in the same proportions*.

For example, eligibility is established if Ms. X and Mr. Y each own 50% of the foreign company (where the L-1 employee has worked for at least a year) and the U.S. company (where the employee will work in L-1 status). However, if Ms. X owns 70% of the foreign company (and Mr. Y owns 30%), and each own 50% of the U.S. company, eligibility as an affiliate cannot be established. In that situation, even though Ms. X and Mr. Y together own 100% of both companies, they do not own them in the same proportions, so the companies cannot be considered to be affiliates for the purpose of L-1 classification. The solution in that case may be to make one company a *subsidiary* of the other (by reorganizing so one company owns the stock of the other).

L-1 employees are either managers or executives (L-1A), or those with "specialized knowledge" of the company's products, services or procedures (L-1B).

A "manager" usually supervises other employees, but it may be possible to qualify as a "manager" by managing an important company function. For example, the CFO of a small corporation might not supervise any other accountants, but probably would still qualify as a manger if she is solely responsible for the company's accounting functions. The ability to hire and fire other employees (or help to make those types of personnel decisions) is usually an important factor in determining L-1A eligibility. If L-1A eligibility is based primarily on the supervision of other employees, those other employees must either be 1) "professional" employees (normally those with college degrees), or 2) managers who in turn supervise others.

The USCIS often takes a restrictive view as to whether an employee possesses company-specific "specialized knowledge" that would justify an L-1B visa. Generally, to qualify in this category the employee must have worked for the company for several years (not just the minimum one-year eligibility period) and have essential knowledge that is not generally held throughout the company.

The "Blanket" L-1

Large companies can submit one "blanket" L-1 petition (to establish the requisite corporate relationship between the U.S. *receiving company* and the foreign *sending company*). Once the blanket L-1 petition is approved, an individual petition is no longer required for each employee. Instead, they apply for the L-1 visa directly to the U.S. Embassy or Consulate abroad, with documents that prove their eligibility as a manager or a person with "specialized knowledge".

A company is eligible for blanket L-1 approval if it has:

1) U.S. sales of more than $25 million,
2) 10 individual L-1 petitions approved over the past year, or
3) at least 1,000 U.S. employees.

A blanket petition is initially approved for three years, and can then be extended indefinitely.

E-1 and E-2 Visas – A Better Alternative to H's and L's?

E-1 and E-2 visas should always be explored if your U.S. company is at least 50% owned by a foreign corporation or foreign individuals. If your company is publicly traded on a U.S. stock exchange, or is owned by American citizens, your employees probably are not eligible for an E visa, and you can skip this chapter.

However, there are many companies in the U.S. that are owned by foreign nationals, or that are subsidiaries for foreign corporations, and you may work for one of them. In that case you should consider the E-1 or E-2 visa for your employees.

Eligible E-1 and E-2 Countries

Eligibility for E-1 and E-2 visas is based on treaties. Currently, the U.S. has E-1 and E-2 treaties with the following countries:

Country	Classification	Effective Date
Albania	E-2	January 4, 1998
Argentina	E-1	October 20, 1994
Argentina	E-2	October 20, 1994
Armenia	E-2	March 29, 1996
Australia	E-1	December 16, 1991
Australia	E-2	December 27, 1991
Austria	E-1	May 27, 1931
Austria	E-2	May 27, 1931
Azerbaijan	E-2	August 2, 2001
Bahrain	E-2	May 30, 2001
Bangladesh	E-2	July 25, 1989
Belgium	E-1	October 3, 1963
Belgium	E-2	October 3, 1963
Bolivia	E-1	November 09, 1862
Bolivia	E-2	June 6, 2001
Bosnia and Herzegovina	E-1	November 15, 1882
Bosnia and Herzegovina	E-2	November 15, 1882
Brunei	E-1	July 11, 1853
Bulgaria	E-2	June 2, 1994
Cameroon	E-2	April 6, 1989
Canada	E-1	January 1, 1993
Canada	E-2	January 1, 1993
Chile	E-1	January 1, 2004
Chile	E-2	January 1, 2004
China (Taiwan)	E-1	November 30, 1948
China (Taiwan)	E-2	November 30, 1948

Colombia	E-1	June 10, 1848
Colombia	E-2	June 10, 1848
Congo (Brazzaville)	E-2	August 13, 1994
Congo (Kinshasa)	E-2	July 28, 1989
Costa Rica	E-1	May 26, 1852
Costa Rica	E-2	May 26, 1852
Croatia	E-1	November 15, 1882
Croatia	E-2	November 15, 1882
Czech Republic	E-2	January 1, 1993
Denmark	E-1	July 30, 1961
Ecuador	E-2	May 11, 1997
Egypt	E-2	June 27, 1992
Estonia	E-1	May 22, 1926
Estonia	E-2	February 16, 1997
Ethiopia	E-1	October 8, 1953
Ethiopia	E-2	October 8, 1953
Finland	E-1	August 10, 1934
Finland	E-2	December 1, 1992
France	E-1	December 21, 1960
France	E-2	December 21, 1960
Georgia	E-2	August 17, 1997
Germany	E-1	July 14, 1956
Germany	E-2	July 14, 1956
Greece	E-1	October 13, 1954
Grenada	E-2	March 3, 1989
Honduras	E-1	July 19, 1928
Honduras	E-2	July 19, 1928

Iran	E-1	June 16, 1957
Iran	E-2	June 16, 1957
Ireland	E-1	September 14, 1950
Ireland	E-2	November 18, 1992
Israel	E-1	April 3, 1954
Italy	E-1	July 26, 1949
Italy	E-2	July 26, 1949
Jamaica	E-2	March 7, 1997
Japan	E-1	October 30, 1953
Japan	E-2	October 30, 1953
Jordan	E-1	December 17, 2001
Jordan	E-2	December 17, 2001
Kazakhstan	E-2	January 12, 1994
Korea (South)	E-1	November 7, 1957
Korea (South)	E-2	November 7, 1957
Kosovo	E-1	November 15, 1882
Kosovo	E-2	November 15, 1882
Latvia	E-1	July 25, 1928
Latvia	E-2	December 26, 1996
Liberia	E-1	November 21, 1939
Liberia	E-2	November 21, 1939
Lithuania	E-2	November 22, 2001
Luxembourg	E-1	March 28, 1963
Luxembourg	E-2	March 28, 1963
Macedonia, the Former Yugoslav Republic of (FRY)	E-1	November 15, 1882

Macedonia, the Former Yugoslav Republic of (FRY)	E-2	November 15, 1882
Mexico	E-1	January 1, 1994
Mexico	E-2	January 1, 1994
Moldova	E-2	November 25, 1994
Mongolia	E-2	January 1, 1997
Montenegro	E-1	November 15, 1882
Montenegro	E-2	November 15, 1882
Morocco	E-2	May 29, 1991
Netherlands	E-1	December 5, 1957
Netherlands	E-2	December 5, 1957
Norway	E-1	January 18, 1928
Norway	E-2	January 18, 1928
Oman	E-1	June 11, 1960
Oman	E-2	June 11, 1960
Pakistan	E-1	February 12, 1961
Pakistan	E-2	February 12, 1961
Panama	E-2	May 30, 1991
Paraguay	E-1	March 07, 1860
Paraguay	E-2	March 07, 1860
Philippines	E-1	September 6, 1955
Philippines	E-2	September 6, 1955
Poland	E-1	August 6, 1994
Poland	E-2	August 6, 1994
Romania	E-2	January 15, 1994
Serbia	E-1	November 15,1882
Serbia	E-2	November 15,1882

Senegal	E-2	October 25, 1990
Singapore	E-1	January 1, 2004
Singapore	E-2	January 1, 2004
Slovak Republic	E-2	January 1, 1993
Slovenia	E-1	November 15, 1882
Slovenia	E-2	November 15, 1882
Spain	E-1	April 14, 1903
Spain	E-2	April 14, 1903
Sri Lanka	E-2	May 1, 1993
Suriname	E-1	February 10, 1963
Suriname	E-2	February 10, 1963
Sweden	E-1	February 20, 1992
Sweden	E-2	February 20, 1992
Switzerland	E-1	November 08, 1855
Switzerland	E-2	November 08, 1855
Thailand	E-1	June 8, 1968
Thailand	E-2	June 8, 1968
Togo	E-1	February 5, 1967
Togo	E-2	February 5, 1967
Trinidad & Tobago	E-2	December 26, 1996
Tunisia	E-2	February 7, 1993
Turkey	E-1	February 15, 1933
Turkey	E-2	May 18, 1990
Ukraine	E-2	November 16, 1996
United Kingdom	E-1	July 03, 1815
United Kingdom	E-2	July 03, 1815
Yugoslavia	E-1	November 15, 1882

| Yugoslavia | E-2 | November 15, 1882 |

Source: Department of State Website[12]

For both E-1 and E-2 visas, the employer must be owned by nationals of one of these countries, *and the employee must be a national of the same country*. For example, the U.S. subsidiary of Sony or Toyota can hire Japanese nationals in E-1 or E-2 status.

For large companies, there is little effective difference between the E-1 and E-2 category. E-1 visas are for companies that have a large volume of trade with the treaty country (at least 50% of the total trade volume). E-2 visas are for companies that have made a substantial investment in the U.S. Often a company (for example, Sony or Toyota) qualifies for both.

E-1 and E-2 employees are almost identical to L-1 employees. They are either managers or executives, or are "key employees". A "key employee" is someone who "possesses skills essential to the firm's operations in the United States", and therefore is similar (but not the same) as an L-1B employee with "specialized knowledge." Spouses of E-1 and E-2 employees are eligible to work (unlike spouses of H-1B employees, who are not).

Often foreign-owned U.S. businesses overlook E-1 and E-2 visas, and obtain H-1B and L-1 visas instead. However, a

---

[12] I have included the entire list of treaties that provide for E status, and the dates they were enacted, not only because this information may be useful, but also because it is very interesting. For example, our oldest commerce treaty is with Great Britain, signed shortly after the War of 1812. The treaty with Croatia was signed in 1882, but the treaty with Italy was not signed until 1949. We do not have a treaty of commerce and friendship with Portugal, but do with most other European countries, *and with Iran*!

potential employee may be simultaneously eligible for E-1, E-2, H-1B, and L-1 visas, so it is important for the HR manager to understand the relative advantages of these visas to provide appropriate oversight to the company's immigration attorney. E-1 and E-2 visas can be easier and cheaper than H-1B visas, and can avoid some of the eligibility problems associated with L-1B visas. Advantages over H-1B visas include the following:

1. There is no petition to the USCIS. Instead the E visa is adjudicated at the U.S. Embassy or Consulate abroad. Avoiding the USCIS also avoids:
    a. High H-1B USCIS filing fees (usually $2,325 for each petition).
    b. USCIS processing times (several months, or an additional $1,225 for "Premium Processing").
2. There is no quota for E-1 and E-2 visas, so employment can start at any time of the year (rather than waiting for October 1 for H-1B status).
3. Unlike the H-1B, the E-1 and E-2 employee does not require a Labor Condition Application (LCA) from the Department of Labor. That provides several advantages to the employer:
    a. A burdensome paperwork requirement is avoided.
    b. The employee does not have to be paid a "prevailing wage".
    c. There is no potential liability for LCA violations (for example, back wages and fines for failing to pay a prevailing wage, or for not properly terminating the employee).
    d. There is no legal requirement to pay for return transportation.
    e. Most importantly, the E-1 and E-2 employee can work anywhere in the U.S., at any salary,

without the necessity of an LCA for each location.

4. E-1 or E-2 employees does not have to have college degrees, or be professionals, to qualify. Instead, they just need to be managers, or have essential company-specific skills.
5. There is no time limit, and often an employee can remain in the U.S. in E status for several decades.
6. Spouses are eligible to work!

L-1 visas also has many of these advantages over the H-1B (most importantly, freedom from the LCA requirement). However, an E-1 or E-2 visa also can have several advantages over an L-1 visa:

1. Many U.S. Embassies (for example, in Tokyo and Manila) permit the company to register just once for E-1 and E-2 visas (much like a blanket L-1 petition). When employees apply for the visas, only evidence relating to the employee (such as job description and background) is required, because all of the company documents (such as formation documents and annual reports) already have been submitted. That can result in a fairly streamlined visa process.
2. The $825 L-1 filing fee paid to the USCIS (or $500 fraud fee paid to the U.S. Embassy in the case of a blanket L-1 petition) is avoided. For example, the entire filing fee paid to the U.S. Embassy in Tokyo for both company registration and E visa issuance is just $390 (which also must be paid by all L-1 and H-1B visa applicants as well).
3. Typically the E visa is issued for a period of five years, compared to an initial period of three years for L-1 visas.
4. There is no time limit on E visas, whereas L-1 visas are limited to 7 years for managers, and 5 years for those with specialized knowledge.

Most importantly, the E-1 or E-2 visa will circumvent the overly-restrictive USCIS interpretation of a "specialized knowledge" (L-1B) employee, and is more likely to be approved. Over the past several years the USCIS has limited "specialized knowledge" in response to perceived abuses of the L-1B category by Indian consulting companies and job shops (India is not an E treaty country -- see list above). Most U.S. Embassies and Consulates are willing to follow State Department guidance for E "key employees." Rather than requiring unique skills as the USCIS often does, the U.S. Embassy will generally focus on several factors such as the following:

1. Degree of proven expertise of the alien in the area of specialization;
2. The uniqueness of the specific skills;
3. The function of the job to which the alien is destined; and
4. The salary such special expertise can command.

For managers and executives, the L-1A visa is usually the better alternative, even if they also qualify for E-1 or E-2 status. Preapproval of the visa petition by the USCIS resolves eligibility issues in advance, so the manager or executive is not burdened with demonstrating that she really is a manager or executive at the time of his or her visa interview at the U.S. Embassy or Consulate.[13]

Although mostly used by large international corporations, E visas can also be used by individual investors and small businesses. E visas are particularly useful for managers or

---

[13] It is generally assumed that only those in L-1A status can apply for permanent residence status as an intra-company transferring manager or executive (EB-1). However, a person can apply for EB-1 classification from any nonimmigrant category as long as he or she meets the EB-1 requirements.

owners of businesses abroad who wish to start a business or subsidiary in the U.S. Often, L-1A visas are not issued for that situation, because the USCIS may conclude that U.S. operations are not large enough to require a manger. That is seldom a problem with E visas, as long as the U.S. company requires a substantial investment, or will carry on substantial trade with the treaty country.

Visitors

U.S. companies often need to bring people to the U.S. to perform business activities for a short period of time. Those activities may last only a few days, or several months, but fall short of actual employment in the U.S.

"Visitor for Business" status (B-1)

The immigration laws provide for "visitor for business" status (B-1 status). Examples of *bona fide* business visitors include:

1. Employees of a subsidiary or parent company abroad who wish to attend business meetings to coordinate corporate strategy, received training, or provide training.
2. Installers who are required to set up machinery or equipment sold by a foreign manufacturer.
3. Representatives of customers, suppliers, or corporate partners abroad who wish to integrate business functions, negotiate contracts, or research in the U.S.
4. Foreign members of the Board of Directors who wish to attend meetings in the U.S.

Nationals of most countries must apply in advance for a B-1 visa at the U.S. Embassy or Consulate in their home countries, and also explain the reason for their visit to the immigration inspector (CBP; "Customs and Border Protection") when they arrive in the

U.S. at the international airport or other port of entry.

Visa Waiver

Nationals of some "Visa Waiver" countries do not need a visa, and only need to explain their mission once, to the CBP officer at the time of admission. Currently the 36 visa waiver countries include the following:

Andorra	Hungary	New Zealand
Australia	Iceland	Norway
Austria	Ireland	Portugal
Belgium	Italy	San Marino
Brunei	Japan	Singapore
Czech Republic	Latvia	Slovakia
Denmark	Liechtenstein	Slovenia
Estonia	Lithuania	South Korea
Finland	Luxembourg	Spain
France	Malta	Sweden
Germany	Monaco	Switzerland
Greece	the Netherlands	United Kingdom

These are mostly developed countries with higher standards of living. It is easier to visit the U.S. without a visa because it is presumed that their citizens want to return to their countries at the end of their visit (rather than remain illegally in the U.S.).

Visa waiver visitors must have a machine-readable passport that is valid for 6 months longer than their expected stay in the U.S. Prior to their departure to the U.S. they must provide information online to the CBP through a system called "ESTA" (https://esta.cbp.dhs.gov/).

Both visitors with visas and visa-waiver visitors must present evidence to the CBP officer on arrival to demonstrate that the purpose of their visit is for valid business reasons and is consistent with Department of State and CBP policy. Some of the primary concerns are:

1. The visit does not involve employment in the U.S.
2. The visitor has permanent ties to his or her home country, and will return.
3. The visitor will not be paid from any U.S. source. (However, travel expenses paid by the U.S. company, including room and board, are permitted.)
4. The visitor will not compete with local employees (i.e., the activity is one that cannot be accomplished through local employment).

For example, you may have an employee of a subsidiary abroad who is a skilled IT worker who you wish to visit to implement a new information system in the U.S. Generally that would be considered to be local employment (even though the worker will continue to be paid abroad) because you could hire a U.S. worker or vendor to perform the implementation. However, if the goal of the implementation is to coordinate the U.S. information system with that of the foreign subsidiary, and the foreign employee has special familiarity with the system, CBP probably would allow the visit.

Business visitors with B-1 visas are allowed into the U.S. for the period of time needed to accomplish their missions, with a maximum allowed time of six months. If the period of six months is insufficient, they can apply to the USCIS to extend their stay for up to an additional six months. Visa Waiver visitors (i.e., those from the countries listed above) are limited to 90 days, and no extension is available. However, even visitors from Visa Waiver countries can get B-1 visas if they have a good reason for claiming that 90 days is insufficient time to accomplish their business objectives.

Employment of Students (F-1)

Foreign students (in F-1 status) are normally allowed to accept employment in the United States for one year after graduating from a U.S. college or university. This period of employment is called "Practical Training" and must be related to the student's major field of study. However, a formal training program is not required, and the "trainee" can perform the same duties as a regular employee.

"Practical Training" is also available before the student finishes his or her academic program, if the employment is part of a college work-study program.

These two periods of employment authorization for F-1 students are designated "Optional Practical Training" (OPT) for post-graduate employment, and "Curricular Practical Training" (CPT) for work-study employment while attending college. An Employment Authorization Document (EAD) issued by the USCIS is required to complete the I-9 for an OPT employee. A notation from the college on the student's "Certificate of Eligibility" (form I-20) is sufficient to establish the right to work and I-9 compliance for a CPT employee (i.e., a separate work authorization from the USCIS is not required).

CPT is relatively rare, and HR managers will mostly encounter OPT for post-graduation employment.

OPT

Because graduation from college is a requirement for OPT, most employees who begin OPT employment will also be eligible for H-1B classification as a "professional." The one year of employment authorization provides employers with an opportunity to evaluate the employee before investing in H-1B sponsorship, but it is a good idea to start the process of changing to H-1B status well in advance of EAD expiration. Although a petition to change status from F-1 (student) to H-1B can be filed at any time before the EAD expires (and 60 days thereafter), the quota may make H-1B visas unavailable for the current fiscal year (*see*, the discussion of H-1B status in Chapter 1), and most H-1B petitions for students therefore should be prepared and filed by April 1. USCIS rules permit filing the H-1B petition six months before its effective date, April 1 is the earliest the petition can be filed for employment on October 1, the first day of the government's fiscal year.

If an H-1B petition is filed for the OPT employee before his or her EAD expires, but before the quota is available for the next fiscal year (which begins October 1), the employee is authorized to continue working until October 1. For example, if the EAD expires July 1, and an H-1B petition is filed on April 1 under the quota for the next fiscal year (to begin October 1), the employee's OPT will continue until October 1. This additional period of employment authorization beyond the normal period of one year is called "Cap Gap" relief (the "Cap" refers to the H-1B quota). No additional EAD is issued for this Cap Gap period, but the I-9 can be updated using the receipt (on form I-797) for filing the H-1B petition. In this case, the employment authorization expiration date can be entered on the I-9 as October 1.

Although OPT is normally limited to 12 months, F-1 students in certain "STEM" occupations (those in Science, Technology, Engineering and Math) can extend the employment authorization for 17 months (for a total of 29 months). **This additional 17 months of OPT is available only to F-1 employees who work for employers that have signed up for E-Verify** (see the discussion of E-Verify in Chapter 14). To obtain the STEM OPT extension, the employee must provide information about the employment to the college, which will enter that information into SEVIS ("Student and Exchange Visitor Information System"), the automated database used by the government to monitor students. The employee must then apply for a new EAD on form I-765. Evidence of STEM OPT for I-9 updating will consist of the employee's new EAD. If that is not available, the I-9 can be updated using the form I-20 endorsed by the college with a STEM OPT recommendation and the receipt for the new EAD. If the employee has not yet received the EAD receipt, the I-9 can be updated with just the form I-20 with the STEM endorsement.

A USCIS checklist for applying for OPT status is included on the following page. This checklist can also be found at http://www.ice.gov/doclib/sevis/pdf/opt_checklist.pdf.

F-1 students with OPT will lose their status, including the right to work, if they remain unemployed for 90 days. If they have a 17-month STEM extension, they can remain unemployed up to 120 days.

Traveling While In F-1 Status

Students are best advised not to travel outside the U.S. while they are in OPT status. Either the U.S. Consulate, which issues the F-1 visa, or Customs and Border Protection (CBP), which decides whether to readmit the student into the U.S., may conclude that the student no longer has the required intent to return to his or her home country. Although probably a small risk, the inability to return to the U.S. could result in a serious disruption or termination of the employment. That risk all but disappears once the student has changed to H-1B status, so those with OPT should consider postponing their international travel until then.

U.S. Immigration
and Customs
Enforcement

F-1 STUDENT JOB AID FOR ALL NON-STEM OPT APPLICATIONS

Note: This checklist is intended to serve as general guidance on the OPT application process. Your school may have special requirements that are not covered on this checklist. You should always speak with an international advisor at your school regarding OPT or any other benefit associated with your F-1 status.

Step	Action	Completed
1.	If you believe you are eligible for OPT and would benefit from practical training in your field of study, request a recommendation for OPT from an international advisor who is a Designated School Official (DSO) at your school. Your DSO has to recommend you for OPT in SEVIS and provide you with an updated Form I-20 showing the recommendation. You will submit that Form I-20 with the application for employment authorization.	
2.	Complete the Form I-765, Application for Employment Authorization. The Form I-765 and instructions are available on the U.S. Citizenship and Immigration Services (USCIS) Web site (www.uscis.gov) under Immigration Forms.	
3.	Gather all immigration documents and other supporting materials to submit with the application for employment authorization, including the following: • Form I-94 - photocopy of both sides • Valid passport - photocopy of photo page, renewal page if original has expired, and pages showing amendments such as name changes, corrections, etc. • Visa (if applicable) - photocopy of visa page • Photocopies of all Forms I-20 you have been issued • Photocopies of any previous employment authorization documents (EAD) • Two identical photographs (photograph instructions are found on the Form I-765 instructions under Required Documentation) • $340 fee (check or Money Order payable to the U.S. Department of Homeland Security)	
4.	Schedule a meeting with your DSO to receive the updated Form I-20 with OPT recommendation, and to review your application to ensure you have properly completed the Form I-765 and have all of the required supporting documents.	
5.	Make a photocopy of all application materials.	
6.	File the Form I-765 and supporting documents listed in item 3 with the appropriate USCIS Service Center (depending on where you live).	

Important OPT Reminders:
- For pre-completion OPT, you can file the Form I-765 up to 90 days before being enrolled for a full academic year, as long as the OPT will not begin until after you have completed a full academic year. If you have been enrolled for a full academic year, you can file the Form I-765 up to 120 days prior to the requested OPT start date.
- For post-completion OPT, you can file the Form I-765 up to 90 days before your program end date and no later than 60 days after your program end date.
- The Form I-765 must be received by USCIS within 30 days of the date your advisor made the OPT recommendation in SEVIS (see page 1 of the printed Form I-20 for the date).
- If you move and do not provide USCIS with your new address, your EAD will be returned to USCIS. To change your address, submit an online Form AR-11 to USCIS, and ask your DSO to update SEVIS.
- Your OPT employment must be directly related to your field of study and cannot begin until you have the EAD card in hand (and the start date has arrived).
- F-1 status is dependent upon full-time employment or volunteer service while on post-completion OPT. You cannot accrue more than 90 days of unemployment while on post-completion OPT. If you are close to 90 days, consult with your DSO.
- You will need to continue to update your DSO with address changes and changes in employment while on post-completion OPT.

Exchange Visitors (J-1)

The J-1 visa is called an "exchange visitor" visa because it was first conceived during the Cold War of the 1950s as a means of cultural exchange. Originally the J-1 program was administered by the U.S. Information Agency, the same State Department agency that was responsible for Radio Free Europe and other propaganda efforts. The overriding purpose of the visa was, and still is, to bring people to the U.S. for short periods so they can learn first-hand about the customs, language and government of America. The AFS exchange program for students in high schools is a good example of a J-1 program. Today, J-1 visas are used more than any other visa category except for B-1 and B-2 visitor's visas, and are used by trainees, teachers, and scholars, as well as students and interns. The Australian who helps you onto a ski lift may have a J-1 visa, as might a worker at one of the cultural pavilions at Disney World. Most major universities have J-1 programs for visiting scholars and professors, and most foreign post-graduate medical interns and residents are in J-1 status.

Two Year Return Requirement

Many J-1 visas include a restriction that the exchange visitor must return to his or her country for two years before getting another status in the U.S., a throw-back to the original propaganda and diplomatic purpose of the visa. Clearly, the J-1 visa would be less effective for promoting American values abroad if the visitors remained in the U.S.

The possibility of a two-year return restriction therefore should be considered before using a J-1 visa. That restriction could be a result of the nature of the J-1 program (for example, a Fulbright scholarship will always include a two-year return requirement), or may be imposed because the visitor's skills are needed in the visitor's home country. For example, a Nutritionist from Bangladesh would be subject to the two-year return requirement regardless of the type of J-1 program. A long-term plan to import a potential employee for training, and later to petition for another working status such as H-1B, could be frustrated if the employee is subject to the two-year return requirement.

Procedure

Unlike H-1B, L-1 visas, and most other working visas, J-1 visas are not initiated through a petition to the USCIS. Instead, an application is made to a program sponsor that is authorized by the U.S. State Department. The program sponsor typically charges $1,500 to $2,500 per employee. Two program sponsors we have used successfully in the past are the AIC (http://www.internationalexchangecenter.org/) and AIPT (http://www.aipt.org/employers/index.html). Fairly detailed information about the training program must submitted to the program sponsor, including the training objectives, skills to be acquired, and the functional areas or departments in which the trainees will work.

If accepted into the program, the J-1 visitor is issued a form DS-2019, which is submitted to a U.S. Embassy or Consulate, which will then issue the visa. Usually, but not always, the Embassy or Consulate will note on the visa whether the visitor is subject to the two-year return requirement.

Nature of J-1 Employment

Employers normally use J-1 visas for trainees and interns. Although trainees can be engaged in productive work, the primary purpose of the training program must be to enhance the trainees' skills, and to improve their knowledge of American technologies or methodologies. The training or internship must not duplicate the exchange visitor's prior training or work experience, and cannot be used as a substitute for ordinary employment, or displace a U.S. worker.

Trainees must have a related post-secondary degree or professional certificate and one year of work experience in the field, or no post-secondary degree and five years of experience in the field. Interns must be attending college, or have graduated no more than 12 months before their work in the U.S. will begin. Unskilled or casual labor is not permitted. Training programs and internships can be in any of the following fields:

(i)   Agriculture, Forestry, and Fishing;
(ii)   Arts and Culture;
(iii)   Construction and Building Trades;
(iv)   Education, Social Sciences, Library Science, Counseling and Social Services;
(v)   Health Related Occupations;
(vi)   Hospitality and Tourism;
(vii)   Information Media and Communications;
(viii) Management, Business, Commerce and Finance;
(ix)   Public Administration and Law; and
(x)   The Sciences, Engineering, Architecture, Mathematics, and Industrial Occupations.

This list covers most occupations, but some, such as veterinary medicine and patient care, are intentionally excluded.

The maximum period of a training program is 18 months, but training in tourism, hospitality, and agriculture is normally limited to 12 months. The maximum period of an internship (for college students or recent grads) is 12 months.

Many employers turn to J-1 visas to obtain workers who are unable to get working visas such as H-1B or L-1. However, J-1 visas are not simply alternative to working visas, because of the required training component. A J-1 program will work best for a large corporation that wishes to employ many trainees for temporary periods of up to 18 months.

Other Temporary Work Visas

The temporary work visas discussed in the preceding chapters (H-1B, L-1, TN, F-1, J-1, and E) are the most common and useful visas used by employers. However, those visas are mostly limited to professionals (like engineers and teachers) and managers. There are other possibilities in the alphabet soup of nonimmigrant visas:

Temporary Workers (H-2)

H-2 visas are available for nonprofessional, temporary workers. However, there are three major limitations on H-2 petitions. The primary limitation is that the job itself must be truly temporary, such as seasonal employment in a cannery, ski resort, summer golf club, or agriculture. Second, before filing the H-2 petition, the employer must first advertise the job to demonstrate that Americans do not want it (a mini-labor certification). The third limitation is that the H-2 category, like the H-1B category for professionals, is subject to a quota, so at certain times of the year it may not be available.

Temporary visas for agricultural workers are designated H-2A, and other types of temporary workers (such as for seasonal work) are designated H-2B.

Because of the paperwork involved, and the short duration of the employment, the H-2 visa is normally not practical for one employee. However, the H-2 visa may be a good solution for employers with many openings for seasonal employment that cannot be filled with domestic workers.

Outstanding Scientists, Artists, Educators, Businesspeople, and Athletes (O)

An H-1B visa is the logical choice for most professionals, because eligibility depends on just a college degree (or equivalent) and a job that normally requires such a degree. However, if the H-1B quota is filled, an O-1 visa may be a viable alternative. Also, there are many occupations -- such as dancing, athletics, singing, and acting -- that require exceptional talent and training, but do not normally require a college degree.

The O-1 visa requires extraordinary ability in the sciences, arts, education, business, or athletics. It encompasses achievement in a broad range of human endeavor, including the performing arts, fine arts, and culinary arts, as well as essential persons such as set designers, choreographers, conductors and coaches. The O-1 petition must be accompanied by extensive documentation that the worker is truly extraordinary in his or her field. In addition, the petition must include the recommendation of a peer group, labor union, or a person with expertise in the field.

Performers (P)

A "P" visa may be available for entertainers, athletes, artists, and other performers who are 1) internationally recognized, 2) culturally unique, or 3) part of an exchange program. For an athlete, that generally means a contract with a major professional sports team. Other types of **entertainers must be a part of a group** that has an outstanding international reputation. P-1 status is not available to individual performers (other than athletes), but outstanding individual actors, dancers, or musicians may be eligible for an O-1 visa.

Religious Workers (R)

Religious workers have their own nonimmigrant visa category, R-1 (and a special category for immigrant visas as well [EB-4]). The religious worker category includes not only ministers, but also any occupation that involves a traditional religious function. The eligibility bar is quite low, and only requires membership in the religious denomination for at least two years.

Cultural Workers (Q)

Teachers, performers and artists who convey the culture, history and traditions of their home countries may be eligible for Q-1 visas for up to 15 months. The Q-1 category may include jobs as diverse as a teacher in a French school or a belly dancer in a Moroccan restaurant.

Taxation of Temporary Foreign Workers

Students and Exchange Visitors

One of the advantages of Practical Training (OPT or CPT) status for students and trainees in F-1, J-1, and M-1 status is that they are usually not subject to withholding for social security and Medicare ("FICA"). (Cultural workers in Q status may also be exempt). That is a savings of 6.2%[14] of salary for employees, and another 6.2% for employers (a total of 12.4% of salary!). These workers are exempt from FUTA taxes as well.

There is no requirement to apply to the IRS for this exemption (as there is for religious workers); it is simply available to workers in F-1, J, M-1 and Q status by operation of law (**if** you know about it!). If your company erroneously withholds FICA for these employees when it is not required, you can later adjust your payroll to reverse the company payment, and the employee can claim a refund on IRS form 8316.

Understanding the FICA exemption for these workers can be tricky. The starting point is Section 3121(b)(19) of the Internal Revenue Code (IRC), which provides for the FICA exemption for "a **nonresident alien** individual for the period he is temporarily

---

[14] Temporarily 4.2% in 2011.

present in the United States as a nonimmigrant under subparagraph (F), (J), (M), or (Q) of section 101(a)(15) of the Immigration and Nationality Act, as amended, and which is performed to carry out the purpose specified in subparagraph (F), (J), (M), or (Q), as the case may be".

The key term in this statute is "nonresident alien". It is highly confusing because "nonresident alien" is a tax term, defined in the IRC, and is not an immigration term. Not all "nonimmigrants" (i.e., those in a "lettered" immigration category) are tax "nonresidents."

A tax "resident" is either 1) a U.S. citizen or green card holder, or 2) a person who is physically present in the U.S. for more than half a year (183 days).[15] Those nonimmigrants who are resident in the U.S. for less than half a year are tax "nonresidents" and their income is subject to a different tax. For that reason many people in nonimmigrant status (such as investors in E-2 status), choose to spend less than half their time in the U.S. (so they are not subject to tax on their foreign income).

This qualification that the FICA exemption only extends to "nonresidents" would seem to gut the exemption entirely, since most students pursue their studies for several years in the U.S. before they begin their employment as Practical Trainees. That is, they normally remain in the U.S. for more than half a year each year. However, the definition of a nonresident alien also extends to F, J, M and Q students who have been present in the U.S. for less than five calendar years,[16] and J and Q trainees and teachers (usually) for less than two calendar years.[17] Also, the exemption extends to **students** (but not trainees and teachers) even beyond five

---

[15] A more exact calculation of this "substantial presence test" can be found in the form 1040NR instructions.

[16] IRC section 7701(b)(5)(D), (E).

[17] IRC section 7701(b)(5)(C), (E).

years if "such individual does not intend to permanently reside in the United States" and is complying with all requirements of his or her student status. That should include almost all students who work for your company as Practical Trainees (in OPT or CPT status, as discussed in Chapter 6). In fact, an intent to return to one's home country is a *requirement* for maintaining student status. However, students who have applied for permanent residence status can no longer be treated as tax nonresidents after five years in student status.

The bottom line then is that almost all students in F-1 and M-1 Practical Training status are exempt from FICA withholding, even if they have been in that status for several years. That may be a compelling reason to delay changing the status of an F-1 employee to H-1B status for as long as possible, especially those STEM students who are eligible for an additional 17 months of Practical Training (*see*, Chapter 6).

On the other hand, trainees and teachers in J and Q status lose their nonresident tax status (and therefore their FICA exemption) after two years (four years if he or she is paid by a foreign employer). Since J-1 trainee programs are usually 18 months, and internships 12 months, most people in J-1 status are also exempt from FICA and FUTA.

Often spouses of J-1 and Q students, trainees or teachers (in J-2 or Q-2 status) are eligible to work and are issued an EAD (Employment Authorization Document) by the USCIS. Generally, those spouses are *NOT* exempt from the FICA and FUTA taxes, and are tax residents (because they themselves are not students, trainees or teachers).

Withholding For Tax Nonresidents

As tax nonresidents, employees who are exempt from FICA and FUTA under the above rules, as well as those who spend less than half their time in the U.S., are also subject to different tax rules, and will file form 1040NR or 1040NR-EZ (rather than 1040 or 1040-EZ like everyone else). They should be directed to IRS publication 519 (which explains in detail this separate taxation regime) or to accountants who are experts in this area. It is probably a good idea for employers and their HR representatives to avoid giving any kind of tax advice to employees, beyond the communications necessary to determine the social security and Medicare tax exemptions, and proper income tax withholding.

Tax nonresidents such as students should indicate their nonresident tax status on form W-4 (the tax form that all new employees must fill out when they are hired). The following amounts should be added to the normal amount withheld based on filing status and withholding allowances claimed:[18]

Payroll Period	Add Additional
Weekly	$ 40.40
Biweekly	$80.80
Semimonthly	$87.50
Monthly	$175.00
Quarterly	$525.00
Semiannually	$1,050.00
Annually	$2,100.00

Students and trainees from India are not subject to this additional withholding.

Tax Treaties

The taxation of foreign workers may also be governed by tax treaties with the workers' home countries. Normally these tax treaties will not affect withholding or taxation for most workers in nonimmigrant status. A summary of these treaties can be found in IRS publication 901.

---

[18] See IRS Publication 15.

Totalization Agreements

Another group of nonimmigrant workers who may be exempt from FICA are those from countries that have "totalization agreements" with the U.S. These agreements are designed to prevent double taxation for social security (in the U.S. and in the worker's home country). Currently, the U.S. has totalization agreements with the following countries:

Australia	France	Norway
Austria	Germany	Poland
Belgium	Greece	Portugal
Canada	Ireland	South Korea
Czech Republic	Italy	Spain
Chile	Japan	Sweden
Denmark	Luxembourg	Switzerland
Finland	Netherlands	United Kingdom

A summary of these totalization agreements can be found on the Social Security Administration website at: http://www.ssa.gov/international/agreements_overview.html.

Typically, a worker from one of these countries, who works in the U.S. temporarily (usually five years or less) is not required to pay social security taxes, but is required to pay (and the employer must withhold and also pay) Medicare and Supplemental Security Income (SSI) taxes. For the totalization agreement to apply, normally the employee must be transferred by his or her home country employer to work for an office, affiliate, parent or subsidiary of that company in the U.S. Many employees in L-1 and E status therefore may be exempt from social security tax and withholding.

The employer normally does not have to worry about totalization agreements, but can rely on a "Certificate of Exemption" that the employee obtains from his or her home country social security (or equivalent) office. However, it may be helpful for the HR manager to remind the employee (and company tax advisor) that a transferee from one of the totalization countries may be exempt from Social Security withholding.

Conclusion

Each situation must be analyzed separately, but generally those in F-1 and J-1 status are tax nonresidents who are not subject to FICA and FUTA withholding and tax. Those with other types of working visas (such as L-1) may be exempt from social security withholding if they present a Certificate of Exemption from their home country. Avoiding these taxes can represent a significant savings for both employer and employee.

Labor Certification

Introduction

The preceding chapters have dealt primarily with temporary working visas for foreign employees. However, most of those employees will also want company sponsorship for their permanent residence status ("green card"). Most employment-based green cards start with a labor certification.

Essentially, a labor certification is a determination by the Department of Labor ("DOL") that there is a shortage of U.S. workers who are available for the job proposed for the applicant. This determination of a labor shortage is based on recruitment conducted by the employer before filing the labor certification application. As with an H-1B petition, the labor certification can be approved only if the employer establishes that it will pay the "prevailing wage," usually a weighted average of salaries for similar positions in the area of intended employment.

Many HR managers struggle with the question of when to begin green card sponsorship. Certainly there is no immediate benefit for the employer, since most employees who request green card sponsorship are already working for the employer in one of the "letter" categories discussed in the previous chapters. However, if the employer does not support a labor certification and eventually a green card, the employee is likely to start looking for another employer that will.

A common compromise (between the employee's anxiety to become a permanent resident and the employer's reluctance to spend the money to make that happen) is to start the green card case after the employee has worked for the company for one year. Employees are unlikely to change employers if they know that the present employer will support the green card process within a year, and after one year employers will know whether they want to keep the employee for a permanent position.

The DOL's goal in the labor certification process is to protect American workers from undue foreign competition (and not to make it easy for immigrants to get green cards). This role focuses on making sure that 1) qualified U.S. workers are not displaced by the foreign worker, and 2) the employment of the foreign worker does not depress the wages and working conditions of U.S. workers. The labor certification process ensures that a competitive salary is paid, and that the job is made available to American workers at that salary.

Generally, labor certifications for engineers, scientists, and other highly skilled workers will be approved, and those for jobs that are attractive to American workers (such as CEO positions), or that do not require special education or experience, will not be approved.

The first concern of the HR manager is to determine whether it is even worthwhile to begin a labor certification. That determination can be based on your own assessment of the job market, and the opinion of the immigration attorney. However, there may be other considerations, including the total cost of the undertaking, strategic considerations for extending H-1B status beyond the six-year limit, and employee relations. For example, it may make sense to begin a case that has a low probability of success because the employee may look for a job somewhere else if you do not. Generally though you will not want to start a case that does not have a very good chance of success, and in any event, it is important to assess the chances of success so you know whether the investment is cost-effective.

The essential components of a successful labor certification include the following:

- **U.S. Job** – Must have a job or offer for full-time employment in the U.S. The job offer must be in good faith (that is, the immigrant must plan to work in that job indefinitely after getting the green card).
- **Willing Employer** – The employer must be motivated and the HR manager must have the time to do all that is required to provide sponsorship, such as place and pay for ads, interview applicants, post notices, keep records, and sign forms.
- **Competitive Salary** – The employer must also be willing to pay a competitive salary. This salary is generally the weighted average of the salaries of those in similar jobs in the city or county where the job will be located. The immigration attorney can give you a rough idea of what this "prevailing wage" may be, but ultimately it is up to the DOL to make this determination based on the job description and job requirements you describe.
- **Skilled Job** – The requirements for the job generally should include at least **two years** of training, experience **or** education to avoid the chronically backlogged "Other Workers" immigration category.
- **Shortage of Qualified U.S. Workers** – There cannot be any qualified U.S. workers who 1) respond to the recruitment ads **and** 2) are willing to take the job.

Costs

A major cost of the labor certification case is the legal fee, which may range from $5,000 to $15,000 depending on the law firm you hire and the perceived complexity of the case. The legal fee for the labor certification may or may not also include the legal fees for the subsequent immigrant visa petition (I-140) and green card application ("application for adjustment of status"; I-485). The range of fees for a stand-alone I-140 may be $750 to $2,500, with the same range for the I-485 for each family member who applies for the green card.

Another cost is your own administrative time in processing the labor certification. Usually the HR department's role consists of the following:

1) providing a job description,
2) consulting with the employee's manager to define the minimum job requirements,
3) reviewing and signing applications,
4) conducting the recruitment of U.S. workers,
5) obtaining evidence of the recruitment, and
6) preparing a report that describes why each applicant could not be hired.

Depending on the effectiveness of your attorney and the nature of the case, the required administrative time can range from just a few hours to a several days or even weeks. As with most things, the best way to reduce the time committed to a labor certification case is to handle these tasks quickly and efficiently. It is best to streamline the process by assigning only one person to handle all aspects of the labor certification (and thus avoid wasteful memos, emails, and meetings to coordinate the case), and that person should work directly with the attorney. If handled correctly, the administrative burden of the labor certification can be fairly light, and involve only two or three hours of your time; if not, the case can drag on for months and become a mire of red tape.

A third cost may be filing fees. In 2011, the DOL does not charge a filing fee for the labor certification, but may soon. *Once the labor certification is approved, an immigrant visa petition (I-140) must be filed within 180 days, or the labor certification will be irrevocably cancelled* (and you would have to start over from the beginning). Currently, the filing fee for the I-140 is $580. The green card application (I-485) fees are $1,070 for each adult applicant, and $635 for each accompanying child under 14 years of age.

DOL regulations require that the employer pay all of the costs of the labor certification, including legal fees and advertising costs, without later reimbursement from the employee. However, the employee can pay all costs associated with the I-140 and I-485, including the USCIS filing fees. Often employers arrange to split the fees and costs with the employee, as permitted by those regulations.

Who can Benefit from a Labor Certification?

An employer can file a labor certification for a potential employee even if he or she is not currently working for your company and even if currently outside the U.S. To benefit from labor certification, an employee must be one of the following:

- In valid, unexpired nonimmigrant status (such as H-1B status); or
- Last entered the U.S. in F-1 (student) or J-1 (exchange visitor) status (even if out of status or working without authorization)[19]; or

---

[19] Those in F-1 or J-1 status who worked without authorization for more than 180 days cannot adjust status, but <u>can</u> seek consular processing, and are not subject to INA 212(a)(9)(B) inadmissibility for unlawful presence.

- In the U.S. out of status, but entered the U.S. legally and did not a) stay in the U.S. past the expiration date on the I-94 or b) work without authorization, for more than 180 days; or
- In Temporary Protected Status (TPS) or eligible for TPS status (for example, those from El Salvador, Nicaragua or Honduras) (even if previously out of status for more than 180 days, worked without authorization, or entered without inspection); or
- Filed a valid labor certification application, *whether or not approved, denied or withdrawn*, before April 30, 2001 (even if previously out of status for more than 180 days, worked without authorization, or entered the U.S. without inspection); or
- Filed a valid immigrant visa petition (I-130, I-140, I-360 or I-526), *whether or not approved, denied or withdrawn*, before April 30, 2001 (even if previously out of status for more than 180 days, worked without authorization, or entered the U.S. without inspection);
- The spouse of someone who filed a valid labor certification application or immigrant visa petition before April 30, 2001, *even though no longer married to that spouse*; or
- Outside of the U.S. and never stayed in the U.S. illegally for more than 180 days (except in F-1 or J-1 status); or
- Outside of the U.S. and stayed in the U.S. illegally for more than 180 days but 1) only stayed illegally before April 1, 1997, 2) stayed less than a year but subsequently stayed outside of the U.S. for at least three years, or 3) stayed more than a year but subsequently stayed outside of the U.S. for at least ten years; or
- Applied for political asylum while still in status, and did not work for more than 180 days without authorization.

In most cases, the employee will simply be in a temporary working status like H-1B, L-1B, or E-2. However, there may be rare cases where you cannot hire the employee temporarily (because he or she is out of status), but can sponsor the labor certification and green card.

Labor Certification Procedure

Regulations issued December 27, 2004 (called "PERM"), require employers to conduct recruitment without government supervision *before* filing the labor certification application. (Before then, recruitment could be conducted either before filing, or after filing under government supervision.) An online application is then prepared that summarizes the recruitment conducted and the response (including the number of workers who applied), and it can be filed electronically. After a short period of review, the DOL will approve the application, issue an audit letter, or ask the employer to conduct further recruitment under the supervision of the DOL.

Labor certification recruitment will be easiest for jobs that do not require a college degree (for example, carpenters or cooks). In those cases, required minimum recruitment consists only of a 30-day job order at the state job office (in California, http://www.caljobs.ca.gov) and an advertisement in the major metropolitan newspaper on two different Sundays.

For those jobs that require a college degree, the required recruitment is more extensive. Like the recruitment for the non-professional positions, mandatory recruitment includes a 30-day job order and two Sunday newspaper ads (although in some cases an ad in a professional journal can take the place of one of the Sunday ads). In addition, the employer must conduct *three* of the following types of additional recruitment:

1. An ad on the newspaper's website (usually the newspaper will run a web-based ad for no additional charge in conjunction with the required Sunday ads).

2. An ad on the employer's own website.

3. An ad in a newsletter or journal published by a trade organization.

4. Local or ethnic newspaper (in addition to Sunday ads in major metropolitan newspaper).

5. Placement agency (headhunter).

6. Campus recruitment.

7. Campus placement office.

8. Employee referral program with incentives.

9. An independent job search website. (Generally, large commercial job search websites such as Monster.com are not very useful because they often yield hundreds of résumés, with many submissions generated automatically.)

10. Job fair.

The recruitment must be conducted no more than 6 months, and at least 30 days, before filing the application.

The offered salary does NOT need to be included (and therefore normally should not be included) in any of the recruitment media listed above. However, there is a "Notice of Filing" that the attorney will prepare that must be posted at the place where the employee will work (and that other employees will be able to see). Often, the offered salary can be disguised somewhat on the Notice of Filing by using a salary range. The lower end of that range must be at least the prevailing wage, and the top end is usually the offered salary (e.g., $97,394 to $120,000).

Audits

In all cases the DOL will make sure that the employer exists and has employees. As soon as the application is filed, the DOL will send an email to the HR manager asking for confirmation that the job offer exists and that the employer in fact filed the application.

In addition, a few cases will be selected for audit. The application itself may trigger the audit based on the DOL's selection criteria, or the audit may be random. If the employer is a closely held corporation, or if the employee is one of a small number of employees, the audit response must also demonstrate that the job is a bona fide job opportunity.

Like a tax return, a labor certification application is processed on a "post-audit" basis. That is, it may be approved (just like your tax refund is issued), but the DOL can audit and disallow the labor certification at any time within five years of the approval.

Many labor certification applications are also audited *before* approval. Two major areas of inquiry in both pre- and post-approval audits are 1) whether the minimum job requirements are excessive, and 2) whether U.S. workers were improperly rejected.

Minimum Job Requirements

The minimum job requirements will be used to determine if any of the applicants who respond to the required recruitment are qualified for the job to be certified. Because the minimum requirements can be used as a basis for rejecting U.S. workers, they are subject to particular scrutiny by the DOL. In addition, there have been many administrative appellate decisions that discuss whether specific job requirements are justifiable.

There are many aspects to the DOL consideration of the minimum job requirements, including the following:

1. Each requirement must be justified in terms of "business necessity." Business necessity essentially requires that the required background is necessary in order for an employee to adequately perform the job duties.

2. The requirements cannot be "tailored" to the immigrant's background, but must reflect the company's actual, normal minimum requirements for the job.

3. There should be consistency with past labor certification applications for the same position (otherwise the DOL could conclude that the employer is not honestly stating its normal job requirements).

4. Minimum requirements cannot include skills that can be learned after a short period of on-the-job training.

5. The requirements cannot be subjective, but must provide an objective measure that can be applied to the job applicants who respond to the recruitment. A requirement like "good communication skills" would not be acceptable.

6. Only the most important skills can be included as minimum requirements. The DOL will normally reject a long list of technical requirements.

7. An ability to speak a foreign language is rarely acceptable. However, there may be an exception where the employee will speak that language most of the time, or where there are safety reasons for the

language (such as to provide safety training to other employees who do not speak English).

8. The employer must certify that it has not previously hired workers for a comparable position with less education and experience.

In most cases, the sponsored immigrant must also be able to prove that he or she met each of the minimum requirements *before* starting the job to be certified. Ordinarily that proof consists of letters from former employers and college transcripts. Proof that the immigrant meets the minimum requirements must be gathered before filing the labor certification, and ideally before starting the recruitment. Otherwise the employer runs the risk of wasting time and money to get a labor certification that cannot be turned into a green card because the employee cannot get proof of required prior experience.

Much of a proper analysis of the minimum requirements comes down to common sense. The DOL will attempt to determine whether the requirements are reasonable, or whether they are fabricated solely to prove that only the immigrant employee is qualified.

Rejecting Job Applicants

The minimum requirements will be applied to potential candidates who respond to the ads to determine whether they are qualified. However, the job requirements are not the only measure of whether they are qualified. The regulations permit rejection of candidates for any "lawful job related reason." In addition to failure to meet the minimum (and justifiable) job requirements, the following reasons may be sufficient to reject a candidate:

1. The candidate does not have a permanent right to remain in the U.S. That would include those who

have only a temporary right to work in a nonimmigrant status such as F-1, H-1B, or L-1 status. It would also include those who are out of status, or who have applied for but have not been granted a permanent status. Only U.S. citizens, permanent residents, political asylees, and refugees need be considered. Everyone else can be summarily rejected, without inquiry into whether or not they are qualified to do the job. That should therefore be the first question asked. To avoid potential liability for discrimination, the form of the question should be, "Do you have the right to work *permanently* in the United States?"

2. The applicant is no longer interested in the job after finding out more about it. However, employers must be careful about discouraging qualified U.S. workers.

3. The applicant wants a higher salary than that offered. However, the employer cannot assume that the applicant will not accept the salary offered simply because he or she has commanded a higher salary in the past, or has qualifications that exceed the minimum requirements. The applicant should be asked, "Would you accept the job at this salary?"

4. The applicant cannot produce adequate references (if the employer normally requires references), or cannot pass a drug test (if the employer normally conducts such tests).

5. The applicant has a criminal background, or has been fired for poor performance.

There may be other lawful reasons for rejecting a candidate, and those must be determined on a case-by-case basis. Essentially, the recruitment must be conducted in good faith.

That means that all applicants must be considered, and cannot be rejected unfairly. All interviews and other interaction with the applicants should be conducted with the expectation that the DOL will contact the applicant to determine whether he or she was fairly considered for the position, and not discouraged from accepting the job.

Generally, all applicants should be interviewed. If they are not interviewed the DOL may conclude that they were not fairly considered. Interviews do not have to be conducted in person, but may be by telephone. The interviews do not have to be long, and often can be just minute or two (for example, long enough to determine that the applicant does not have the right to work permanently in the U.S.). It is usually not proper to reject a candidate based on the résumé alone because the DOL assumes that the résumé may not include all of the background and qualifications of the candidate. However, in some circumstances, such as where it is clear that the candidate does not have a required college degree, or lacks sufficient experience, a determination can be made without an interview and based on the résumé alone. Notes should be kept of the time, date and content of the interviews.

Good faith recruitment also involves contacting applicants as soon as possible, ideally within a day or two of receiving the résumé or letter of application. The labor certification can be denied if a qualified applicant is not contacted quickly, because it is unreasonable for a job applicant to wait several weeks for a response. The applicant will assume that the job is no longer available, and will seek other opportunities.

If the applicant cannot be reached by telephone or email, a letter should be send to the address on the résumé as soon as possible by certified mail. That letter should provide a telephone number, times and days to call, and ask the applicant to contact the HR manager by telephone. A copy of the certified letter (and certified mail receipt) should be retained for submission in case there is an audit.

Labor Certification Approval Can Be Revoked At Any Time

PERM regulations provide for revoking an approved labor certification at any time, even after the employee is a permanent resident, if either the DOL or USCIS determine that the labor certification was improperly granted. However, the regulations do **not** provide for any additional penalty or fine for employers, as they do in the H-1B context. Accordingly, an employer does not incur any liability for sponsoring a labor certification, unless there is fraud or false statements in the application, or there is a "pattern or practice" of failing to comply with labor certification requirements.

On the other hand, the immigrant employee potentially faces huge penalties if the labor certification is later revoked. Those penalties could include loss of all status in the U.S. and the necessity of uprooting a settled life in the U.S. to return to the employee's home country. There is no time limit on revocations, so it is theoretically possible for the DOL to revoke a labor certification (and therefore the green cards) of the employee and the employee's family many years after they have become permanent residents.

Other Considerations

Some nonimmigrant employees will use the employment to achieve green card status, and leave for other employment as soon as he or she becomes a permanent resident. That possibility certainly has to be considered before starting a green card, but employee retention must be a separate issue from green card sponsorship. We have many employee clients who continue to work for their sponsoring employers decades after their labor certifications and green cards are approved. As with all employees, good working conditions, promotions, and decent compensation are the best ways to retain immigrant employees. We have found that employers who try to gain too much leverage through the immigration process (for example, by making the immigrant employee work longer hours or paying her less than other employees) will eventually lose that employee. Green card sponsorship is an excellent tool to create long-term good will and loyalty, but should not be used to gain an unfair advantage.

Also, if the employer does not sponsor the labor certification, the employee invariably will change to another employer that will. Often, remaining in the U.S. is the highest immediate priority for the worker (rather than career or compensation), and that worker may remember and appreciate the green card sponsorship for years to come.

Conclusion

The labor certifications process initially may appear to be cumbersome and expensive, and in many cases they can be. However, by fairly defining the minimum job requirements, and efficiently conducting the recruitment, an approved labor certification for a shortage occupation usually can be obtained in less than a year. A successful labor certification will create a life-long benefit for the employee, and will enable hiring and retention of exceptional workers from all over the world.

Permanent Residence for "Priority Workers"

"Priority Workers" is a catch-all phrase for employment-based immigration that does not require a labor certification. I include in this category those in "Employment-Based First Preference" (EB-1), and those who can obtain a waiver of labor certification because their work is in the "national interest" (an EB-2 category). The primary advantages of filing as a priority worker are as follows:

1. A test of the job market (placing ads and interviewing applicants) is not required.
2. There is no quota backlog in the EB-1 category for those from China and India (compared to a backlog of four years or so in the EB-2 category).
3. An applicant whose work is in the "national interest" can qualify for the EB-2 category (and avoid a six-year backlog in the EB-3 category) even if he or she does not have a U.S. Bachelor's degree or its academic equivalent.

The EB-1 category is divided into the following three subcategories:

Transferring Managers and Executives

This subcategory is virtually identical to the L-1A category for nonimmigrants, and most EB-1 immigrants already have L-1A visas (although some may have E visas). The EB-1 applicant must have been a manager or executive for at least one year with the U.S. employer's subsidiary, parent or affiliate company abroad. She must also be employed or have a job offer to be employed by the U.S. company as a manger or executive.

The difficult questions in this type of EB-1 case are similar to those in an L-1A case. Who is a "manager"? Who is an "executive"? Does the U.S. employer have the requisite corporate affiliation with the overseas employer? These issues are discussed in Chapter 3.

There are two differences between EB-1 eligibility and L-1A eligibility. First, the one year of employment abroad must have taken place during the three-year period before the applicant came to the U.S. In contrast, L-1A eligibility depends on a year of employment abroad during the three-year period before *filing* the petition. Second, the petitioner must have been in business in the U.S. for at least a year (whereas an L-1A nonimmigrant can transfer to a new U.S. office).

The EB-1 category is useful for transferring managers and executives because it may be difficult or impossible to obtain a labor certification for those employees. A labor certification requires proof that there is a shortage of U.S. workers who want the job and are qualified to do it. Normally, there are many minimally qualified U.S. workers who want the higher salaries and prestige of executive and top managerial positions. Often, potential applicants may already work in your company, in positions lower on the ladder. Finally, managers and executives are usually searching for upward mobility, and ads for those positions normally encourage an avalanche of résumés.

Outstanding Professors and Researchers

Although normally used by colleges and universities, this EB-1 subcategory can be used for researchers at private companies as well. The basic requirements are:

1) The professor or researcher must be recognized *internationally* as outstanding. Normally this is demonstrated by submitting summaries of scholarly articles, references from other outstanding researchers, and evidence of novel contributions to the academic field.
2) If based on outstanding research, the employer must employ at least three full-time researchers (may include the person applying for the green card).
3) The researcher must have three years of paid, full-time research experience. That can include time spent pursuing a Ph.D. or other degree (as long as the researcher actually gets the degree), and time spent with the petitioning employer.

Evidence accepted by the USCIS to establish "outstanding" ability and international recognition must include two of the following categories of evidence:

1) Prizes and awards.
2) Membership in associations that require outstanding achievements.
3) Published material about the applicant.
4) Evidence as a judge of the work of others in the field.
5) Evidence of original scientific or scholarly contributions to the field.
6) Published articles or books by the applicant.

Extraordinary Ability

This category is similar to the nonimmigrant O category (*see*, Chapter 8), and is reserved for those "in the sciences, arts, education, business, or athletics" who have demonstrated "sustained national or international acclaim." They must be "one of that small percentage who have risen to the very top of the field of endeavor." This is a significantly higher standard than the "outstanding" researcher category described above. Beneficiaries of the Extraordinary Ability category can be movie actors, musicians, professional athletes, and top scientists, and perhaps even the world's best poker players and hot-dog eating champions. Unlike the other EB-1 subcategories, an EB-1 petition does not require employer sponsorship (the beneficiary can self-petition).

"Extraordinary ability" must be established with three categories of evidence, which can be selected from the categories of evidence listed above acceptable to demonstrate "outstanding" ability, plus the additional categories:

7) Display of artistic work (for those claiming extraordinary ability in the arts).
8) Performance in a leading or critical role (for actors).
9) High salary or other remuneration.
10) Commercial success in the performing arts.
11) "Other comparable evidence."

National Interest Waiver

We include in the "Priority Worker" category a person whose work is in the "national interest" (because a labor certification is not required). This waiver of a labor certification in the national interest does not place the applicant in the EB-1 category, where there is no current quota backlog, but in the EB-2 category, where there is a multi-year backlog for those born in India or China. However, it still may be a good option for those from other countries where there is no EB-2 backlog, if they do not have a Bachelor's degree, or wish to petition for their green card without employer sponsorship.

The National Interest Waiver petition is most useful for those who have special skills, but who may not be eligible for a labor certification (because there may be many unemployed workers in his or her field) or who may not have time for a labor certification. The key issue in a National Interest Waiver case is whether the proposed employment really benefits the U.S. nationally (rather than just having a local impact). For example, a person employed for an important government agency like the Department of Defense (DOD) may be doing work in the national interest. Similarly, a person employed by a private company with DOD contracts may be able to demonstrate work in the national interest.

An applicant for a National Interest Waiver must have a job that requires at least a Master's degree (or a Bachelor's degree plus five years of experience), OR must be "exceptional." Although defined in the dictionary in pretty much the same way, for immigration purposes "exceptional" is a much lower standard than the "outstanding" and "extraordinary" categories described above. An "exceptional" person has "a degree of expertise significantly above that ordinarily encountered." Often the USCIS will confuse these standards, and apply the higher "outstanding" or "extraordinary" standard to an EB-2 case. Also, there is a huge subjective component in determining exceptional ability (what exactly does "significantly above" mean?!). However, a properly prepared and advocated National Interest Waiver case can be successful for an employee who is not at the top of his or her field, but who has greater expertise than most people in the field.

Evidence of exceptional ability must include three of the following:

(A) An official academic record showing that the alien has a degree, diploma, certificate, or similar award from a college, university, school, or other institution of learning relating to the area of exceptional ability;

(B) Evidence in the form of letter(s) from current or former employer(s) showing that the alien has at least ten years of full-time experience in the occupation;

(C) A license to practice the profession or certification for a particular profession or occupation;

(D) Evidence that the alien has commanded a salary, or other remuneration for services, that demonstrates exceptional ability;

(E) Evidence of membership in professional associations;

(F) Evidence of recognition for achievements and significant contributions to the industry or field by peers, governmental entities, or professional or business organizations; or

(G) If the above standards do not readily apply to the beneficiary's occupation, the petitioner may submit comparable evidence to establish the beneficiary's eligibility.

As you can see, compared to the documentary requirements for Extraordinary or Outstanding ability, the requirements for demonstrating Exceptional Ability are fairly modest.

Currently, most of the priority worker categories are eligible for "Premium Processing", and USCIS processing can be completed within a week or so. (However, Premium Processing is not yet available for Transferring

Managers/Executives and National Interest Waiver cases, so those will still take several months.)

The priority worker categories should be first examined before starting any employment-based green card case because they enable avoidance of the labor certification process. Although labor certifications in some cases can be completed in just a few months, often they can take years, and in many occupations it may be difficult or impossible to establish a shortage of U.S. workers (always essential to the labor certification case). The priority worker petition bypasses this additional layer of processing and bureaucracy, and in most cases enables immediate application for the green card.

Layoffs and Reductions in Force

A layoff or RIF affects visa employees differently than they affect other workers. Loss of a job may result in loss of the foreign employee's legal status in the U.S. Employers also may have increased liability arising from the termination those in H-1B status.

The impact of a layoff or RIF depends on the type of visa status the worker has, so it is helpful to first make a list of all nonimmigrant employees involved in the RIF, together with their visa status, and the status of any pending labor certification or green card application submitted on their behalf.

Visa Employees

After making that list, the first order of business is to identify those in H-1B status and properly terminate their status (*see*, Chapter 1). Employers have a continuing liability to pay the salary stated on the Labor Condition Application (LCA) and other LCA obligations unless the following four steps are taken:

1. A memorandum or other written communication (like an email) is delivered to the H-1B employee clearing confirming the termination

of employment and the date of termination.

2. The USCIS is notified and the H-1B petition is withdrawn.
3. The LCA is withdrawn with the Department of Labor.
4. An offer is made to the employee to pay the cost of return transportation to the worker's home country.

The company's immigration attorney can assist with withdrawing the H-1B petitions and LCAs.

Visa employees whose status and right to work is specific to the employer include those in H-1B status, L-1 status, E status (usually), O-1, R-1, and J-1.

Those whose status is based on the status of a spouse (and is therefore independent of company sponsorship) include those in L-2 status, E status (those with EADs), and J-2 status.

Employees in F-1 (student Practical Training) status have a right to work that does not depend on a specific employer, but does depend on working in an occupation that is related to his or her college studies.

It is helpful to inform those with a company-sponsored right to work of the impending layoff as soon as possible so they have time to seek other employment that would allow them to remain in the U.S. By doing so you may also avoid liability for the cost of return transportation for H-1B employees. Also, you are less likely to create a disgruntled ex-employee if you partner with them to ease their transition to their next job (and remember: most LCA investigations are triggered by complaints from disgruntled employees; *see*, Chapter 1).

Those in H-1B status are legally able to begin working for a new employer as soon as a new H-1B petition can be filed, and they are not again subject to an H-1B quota. However, if they wait too long before submitting the new H-1B petition, they must leave the U.S. to secure a new visa. Usually (but not always) an employee may remain in the U.S. in H-1B status if the new H-1B petition is filed within 30 days.

Unlike those in H-1B status, workers in the other employer-specific and employer-sponsored visa categories – such as L-1, E-1, E-2, O-1, P-1, J-1, and R-1 – cannot begin working for a new employer as soon as a new petition is filed, but must wait for approval of the petition. Usually the new petition will be an H-1B petition (because they will no longer be eligible for the other categories), and they will be subject to the H-1B quota (unlike someone who is already in H-1B status). If the H-1B quota is filled they may have to wait as much as a year or more before working in the U.S. again. It is therefore even more important that those in the other working categories are able to begin planning for transition to a new company as soon as possible.

Green Card Applicants – "Porting"

The impact of the layoffs on those with pending green card applications depends on how far along in the process they are. Typically, the green card process involves a labor certification (*see*, Chapter 10), an immigrant visa petition (I-140), and an application for adjustment of status (I-485).

For those who have not yet filed an I-485, the loss of the job means that the employee will need to start the process over again with the new employer. However, those whose I-485's has been filed and pending with the USCIS for more than 180 days can "port" (i.e., change employers) and continue with the green card processing using the same approved labor certification and I-140. The only requirement for porting is that the new job is in the same or similar occupation. "Porting" is possible even if the new job is in a different state, commands a lower salary, or even involves self-employment or work as an independent contractor.

Although the statute provides for porting only after 180 days after the I-485 has been filed, it may be possible to take advantage of porting even if the layoff occurs before the 180-day mark (and after filing). That situation can get tricky, and should be analyzed with the immigration attorney.

Those who have an approved I-140, but have not yet filed an I-485 when the layoff occurs, will not be able to port, but will be able to retain the "priority date" (the place in the immigration queue) for a future I-140 for another employer. Those from backlogged quota countries such as China and India are often in this situation. Since most I-140s are eligible for "Premium [Expedited] Processing", the HR manager can assist the employee greatly by making sure that the I-140 gets approved before the layoff occurs. Continuing to pursue the I-140 (which involves an offer of permanent employment) when a RIF is contemplated raises an ethical issue, but I believe that it may be ethical in some circumstances to secure approval of the I-140 before the layoff of that particular employee is finally decided, or if there is a reasonable chance that he or she may be hired back in the future.

Notifying Immigration Attorney

When should you notify the immigration attorney of the planned layoff or RIF? Here, the attorney's dual role as the representative for both the employer and employee should be considered (*see*, Chapter 15). Since the employee's termination will have a significant impact on the employee's immigration status, the attorney probably has an ethical obligation to report this development to the employee. The best approach therefore is to notify the immigration attorney of the layoff or RIF only after the employees have been notified. Unlike the situation of a corporate merger or other restructuring (*see*, Chapter 13), there is no compelling reason for the immigration lawyer to know about the layoff or RIF before the employees know, and withholding that information can keep the attorney out of an awkward ethical dilemma.

In sum, employers must notify the Department of Labor and withdraw the petitions of terminated employees in H-1B and E-3 status (the two employment categories that require a Labor Condition Application [LCA]). Otherwise, LCA liability to pay the employees' salary continues. For all other visa employees, notifying them of the layoff as soon as possible is not required, but might enable them to remain in the U.S. by finding a similar job elsewhere.

Mergers, Acquisitions and Other Corporate Restructuring

Most employment-based immigration petitions are specific to the employer, and are automatically revoked when the employment ends or the employer ceases to exist. A corporate restructuring or merger often results in a new corporate entity. Because the employee works for a new company, he or she may no longer have the legal right to work, and his or her green card case may become derailed. This chapter will explore the effect of a corporate restructuring on employment-based nonimmigrant visas such as H-1B and L-1, as well as its effect on pending employment-based green card cases.

The effect of a corporate restructuring depends on the employee's visa status, and the type of company change. Action should be taken before the merger to maintain the legal status of employees in H-1B (professionals), L-1A (transferring managers), L-1B (transferring workers with specialized knowledge), and TN (Canadian or Mexican professionals) status. Other visa categories that include the right to work – such as F-1 (student status), L-2 (spouse of L-1), J-2 (spouse of J-1), and E-2 (spouse of E-2 principal) – are not based on a specific employer and are not affected by a corporate restructuring.

There are essentially four types of corporate restructuring:

1) Two companies can merge as "equals" (which of course never happens in real life) to form a third company (for example, the ill-fated merger of Chrysler and Mercedes-Benz);
2) An "acquiring" company can swallow up a "target" company, that becomes a part of the acquiring company;
3) A company can purchase the assets (but not the liabilities or employment contracts) of another company; or
4) A company can spin off a division or other part.

Each of these situations demands a different response from the HR manager in order to preserve the legal status and right to work of its nonimmigrant employees. Ideally, this response should be planned and implemented **before** the corporate change, but often the HR manager in charge of visas is presented with the information only after it is completed. In that case, action should be taken as soon as possible.

H-1B Employees

Usually, a new H-1B petition is required if there is any significant change in the employment, such as a change in location, occupation, or employer. However, in the case of most corporate restructurings, the H-1B employees will continue to do the same job, and at the same location, as before the merger. In that case, the new employer (either the acquiring company or new third company) only needs to affirm the obligations of the Labor Condition Application (LCA; *see*, Chapter 1). That affirmation can take the form of a memorandum added to the LCA file in which the new employer assumes those obligations, including payment of the prevailing wage and actual wage.

Often the restructuring can be a problem for H-1B employees because the name of their employer will no longer match the name listed as the employer on their H-1B visas. Immigration inspectors, unaware of these rules, may delay or even deny their reentry into the U.S. because of this discrepancy. The solution is to provide the H-1B employee with a copy of the LCA memorandum and a copy of the law that provides for continuation of the H-1B status despite the restructuring. Those documents can be presented to the immigration inspector in case there is a problem. Some employees will insist on a new H-1B petition and new visa to avoid problems in reentering, but normally that may not be an economical solution considering the costs of a new H-1B petition.

If the acquiring company purchases *only the assets* of the H-1B employer, and does not assume its liabilities and employment contracts generally, the employee is treated as a new hire. In that case, there is no way to avoid the administrative, legal and filing fee costs associated with a new LCA and H-1B petition.

TN Employees

There is no similar rule for those in TN status, so if the restructuring results in a new employer, a new petition must be submitted. There is usually a simple rule for determining whether there is a new employer. If the restructuring results in a new Federal Employer Identification Number (FEIN), it is a new company. For example, if two companies merge to form a new company with a new FEIN, a new petition must be filed. If the employer is acquired, a new petition must be filed. However, if the TN employee works for the acquiring company, a new petition is not necessary because the FEIN will not change.

L-1 Employees

The continued eligibility of those in L-1A and L-1B status also must be analyzed when there is a corporate restructuring. You may recall (*see,* Chapter 3) that L-1 status is based on a corporate relationship between a company the employee worked for abroad, and the employer in the U.S. A restructuring can destroy that corporate relationship, and therefore the original basis for the L-1 status. For example, a U.S. company might acquire another U.S. company, but not its foreign subsidiaries. In that case, the L-1 employees may no longer be working for a company that continues to have any overseas operation, and therefore no longer eligible for continued L-1 status. However, employees can often continue to work in L-1 status, even when there is no longer any corporate relationship with the company abroad on which the L-1 visa was originally based.

L-1 regulations require an amended L-1 petition when there is a company restructuring. The details of the merger or acquisition must be provided to the USCIS, which will make the formal decision as to whether the employee continues to qualify for L-1 status.

If the L-1 status ends because of the restructuring, the employee must leave the U.S., or transfer to another nonimmigrant status like H-1B. Often that can be difficult because the H-1B quota may be filled for the year. It is therefore important to plan ahead, and submit H-1B petitions in plenty of time to avoid interruption in employment because of quota backlogs. That is another reason why it is important to have the HR manager who is responsible for immigration matters, and immigration counsel, to know about the corporate restructuring at the earliest possible time.

Verification of the Right to Work

A primary immigration challenge of HR managers is to make sure that they only employ workers who have the legal right to work. This responsibility is only a quarter century old, imposed by the Immigration Reform and Control Act of 1986 ("IRCA"). The idea behind that legislation was to grant amnesty ("legalization") to those who were in the U.S. illegally, and to end future illegal immigration by ending the jobs magnet. To do that, Congress essentially turned employers into immigration enforcers, a role previously and exclusively held by the Department of Justice. Before 1986 there was no penalty for hiring an illegal alien.

The first goal of IRCA succeeded, and millions of illegal workers and their families were given legal status, and ultimately green cards. However, the second goal, prevention of illegal immigration by shutting down jobs, failed abysmally, and millions more undocumented workers migrated to the U.S. over the next quarter century, some in the hope that Congress would pass another amnesty program (it hasn't). Currently the number of undocumented immigrants in the U.S. is estimated to be roughly 12 million people, over 3% of the population.

IRCA established two separate obligations for employers in its attempt to control illegal immigration, and it is important for HR professionals to be aware of both. First, it made it illegal for an employer to "knowingly" employ an unauthorized worker. Second, it required employers to verify the identity and right to work of each new hire on form I-9. Employers are subject to civil and even criminal penalties for failing to fulfill these obligations.

IRCA failed for the simple reason that undocumented workers obtained and presented to their employers fake documents and fake social security numbers. As long as the documents (showing identity and right to work) appeared to be valid, employers were off the hook and could not be fined for an I-9 violation or for "knowing" that the worker was unauthorized. Also, the regulations that implemented IRCA prevented employers from investigating further, or from "request[ing] more or different documents than . . . required . . . or to refuse to honor documents tendered that on their face reasonably appear to be genuine." Since most phony documents "reasonably appear to be genuine" (which is the entire point of phony documents), there was rarely a basis for refusing to hire a job applicant. Indeed, employers could face liability for discrimination for refusing to hire or conducting an additional investigation because the job applicant appeared to be foreign born.

In addition to checking documents and completing I-9s, HR professionals are responsible for making sure that their companies do not "knowingly" employ those who do not have the legal right to work in the U.S. That involves more than simply complying with the I-9 requirements, and requires further investigation if there is evidence (such as a Social Security "no match letter") that the I-9 documents are fraudulent or the worker is undocumented.

Avoiding Penalties

Civil penalties for knowingly employing an undocumented worker are modest (up to $3,200 per worker for a first offense). However, there are also criminal misdemeanor penalties (fines and up to six months in jail) for a "pattern or practice" of employing undocumented workers.

In a recent attempt to salvage the unsuccessful goals of IRCA, the U.S. Attorney increasingly prosecutes employers *for felonies* if the employer not only knows that a worker is undocumented, but also assists the worker to avoid detection. Employers have been convicted for fraud conspiracy for telling workers to get another fake social security number after receiving a "no match letter", and for "harboring" illegal aliens by providing housing or telling them to "run" when ICE (Immigration Control and Enforcement) officers arrive at the work site. Those felonies are generally punishable by fines and up to five years in prison.

In contrast, mistakes in completing the form I-9 are subject to a "good faith" defense. ICE will give employers a chance to correct technical and procedural errors.[20] Even "substantive violations" carry only modest penalties of between $110 and $1,100 per worker. Also, there are no criminal penalties for I-9 violations, even if there is a "pattern or practice" of such violations. The greatest potential liability for I-9 violations is probably the legal and administrative costs involved in responding to a government investigation and prosecution. That does not mean that responsibility for I-9s can be ignored, but it must be balanced against the greater liability

---

[20] This is known as the "Bono Amendment", 1996 legislation named for Congressperson, musician, and restaurant owner Sonny Bono. "Procedural and technical failures" include such things as failing to provide the employee's address or birth date in Section 1. *Cf.*, March 6, 1997 Virtue Memorandum, and INS Proposed Regulations at 63 Fed.Reg. 16909-13 (April 7, 1998).

for discrimination against those who appear to be foreign-born.

It is a good idea to periodically self-audit the I-9s, to ensure continued compliance. Also, care should be taken to calendar the I-9s of those whose work authorization is temporary, and to make sure that their I-9s are updated or that those employees are removed from the payroll by the time that work authorization expires.

Also, because the penalties for knowingly employing an unauthorized worker are much more severe, it is paramount that workers who clearly do not have the right to work are removed from the payroll. When there is "reason to know" that the employee may be unauthorized, such as a "no-match" letter from the SSA, there is also a duty to investigate, and to terminate the employment if it becomes clear that the employee does not have the right to work.

Discrimination

Discrimination liability in the I-9 process remains an area of serious concern. For example, in 2010, Catholic Healthcare West, America's eighth largest hospital provider, settled discrimination claims with the Civil Rights Division, with penalties exceeding a quarter of a million dollars, for requiring certain documents from foreign-born employees (such as a green card), rather than documents of the employees' own choosing (such as a driver's license and social security card).

Liability for discrimination in the I-9 process can be avoided in the same way that all discrimination claims can be avoided: by implementing procedures that are applied equally to all job applicants. Also, it is important to avoid asking for more documents than those required by federal law.

Although it is always improper to discriminate in hiring against those who are foreign-born, or appear to be foreign-born, it *is* permissible to discriminate against those who are foreign-born *and* who do not have the right to work permanently in the U.S. Those who *cannot* be discriminated against because of their country of birth or citizenship include: 1) green card holders (lawful permanent residents), 2) refugees, 3) political asylees, and 4) U.S. citizens. However, everyone else *can* be discriminated against. Foreign students, those in temporary working status like H-1B, those in "temporary protected status", and those who are waiting for their permanent residence status but do not have it yet, can all be discriminated against in hiring based on their immigration status.

The best way to ask about immigration status to avoid discrimination liability is to ask, "Do you have the right to work permanently in the United States?", since the right to work permanently is granted for green card holders, refugees, political asylees and U.S. citizens, but not for any other immigration status. Another way to ask the same thing, but to make the question more pointed, is to ask, "Are you a lawful permanent resident, refugee, political asylee, or U.S. citizen?" You cannot ask which of those statuses the applicant has, and if he or she simply answers "yes", that should be the end of the discussion. However, often the applicant may volunteer additional information that would affirm or negate the "yes" answer. For example, he may say, "Yes, I am a U.S. citizen", or "Yes, I am married to a U.S. citizen and have my work authorization." The latter answer would enable you (but not require you) to refuse to hire based on immigration status alone. Again, the key is to have a consistent policy that is applied to everyone equally.

E-Verify and Image

E-Verify, the online system for verifying employees' right to work, is one possible tool for avoiding liability for hiring unauthorized workers. Registration for E-Verify can be completed on the USCIS website (www.uscis.gov/everify). Currently it is required for all employers who contract with the U.S. government, and probably within the next few years it will be required for all employers. E-Verify is also required for employers who wish to obtain the 17-month employment authorization extension for STEM college graduates who are working in student Practical Training status (see Chapter 6).

There is also an IMAGE program ("Immigration Control and Enforcement [ICE] Mutual Agreement Between Government and Employers") that involves E-Verify registration and an I-9 audit by ICE (*see*, http://www.ice.gov/image/).

For now, though, the administrative burdens of this voluntary interaction with the government may outweigh its benefits.

Independent Contractors

Often employers believe that they can avoid penalties for hiring an unauthorized worker and avoid the I-9 requirements by making the worker an independent contractor, rather than an employee. However, knowingly hiring an independent contractor who does not have the right to work, carries the same penalties as knowingly hiring an unauthorized employee.[21]

Also, although independent contractors are not subject to the I-9 requirements, they may not really be independent contractors. Whether a worker can be treated as an employee or independent contractor is an issue that HR professionals must deal with in other contexts, but the immigration

---

[21] 8 CFR 274a.1(j)

regulations provide specific guidance in the I-9 context. Factors to be considered include whether the individual or entity:

a) supplies the tools or materials;
b) makes services available to the general public;
c) works for a number of clients at the same time;
d) has an opportunity for profit or loss as a result of labor or services provided;
e) invests in the facilities for work;
f) directs the order or sequence in which the work is to be done and determines the hours during which the work is to be done.

Conclusion

I-9 completion is a fairly simple process that should not consume inordinate resources or time of the HR manager. The only balancing act is making sure that there is a consistent policy so it does not appear that there is discrimination against those who appear to be foreign-born.

The HR manager must navigate potential liability from two different enforcement agencies of the federal government. On the one hand, ICE (Department of Homeland Security) is poised and waiting to strike if the employer fails to complete the I-9 and verify the right to work. On the other, the Civil Rights Division (Department of Justice) seeks to enforce the anti-discrimination provisions of the immigration code. Of these three sources of liability, knowingly employing unauthorized workers is the most serious, followed by discrimination. I-9 liability is limited to civil fines, and there are defenses for good faith violations.

Dual Representation and Other Attorney Issues

Although jokes are often made about the scruples of attorneys, the legal profession is in fact highly regulated and attorneys are subject to extensive ethical rules and guidelines. These ethical constraints are the subject of entire courses in law schools, and are part of every bar examination. Understanding some of those rules can help you deal with your attorney and avoid awkward situations that could arise in connection with the immigration cases.

Most importantly, attorneys have obligations to their clients. Those obligations include at a minimum 1) strict confidentiality, 2) diligence, 3) keeping you informed, 4) competence, and 5) avoiding conflicts of interest that might jeopardize those obligations. As a client in an immigration case, you should expect that those obligations are fulfilled, and should get a new attorney if they are not.

Normally the immigration attorney will represent both the interests of the employer and of the employee. Even if the attorney sets out to represent only the employer (and not the employee), the law will infer an attorney / client relationship if the attorney gives the employee any advice or the employee reasonably believes that the attorney is representing his or her interests. Also, the attorney cannot file any application signed by the employee without entering an appearance as the employee's attorney (on form G-28). That implied attorney / client relationship with the employee can exist even if neither the employer nor the attorney want that relationship, and even though the employee does not pay any part of the legal fee.

If there is an attorney / client relationship with the employee, even if it is only implied, the attorney will have all of the obligations that it has to the employer: confidentiality, diligence, keeping the client informed, competence, and avoiding conflicts of interest.

Normally it is best to have the attorney not only represent your company, but also the immigrant employee. That is because both employer and employee basically want the same thing: to get the working visa or green card as quickly as possible. Also, administration of the cases is improved if the attorney can communicate directly with the employee – to get information and documents, to explain the issues and strategy in the case, and to answer the employee's other immigration questions. Otherwise, the HR manager becomes the go-between, wasting valuable time to sift communications from the lawyer to the employee and back again. The employee may have legal questions that the HR manager is unable to answer, and worse, the employee may begin to pester the HR manager about the status of the case and how much longer it will be before the green card or visa arrives. The attorney should be skilled in fielding those types of questions and providing realistic expectations.

Also, the immigration case is not only a means to get and keep hard-to-find employees, it is also an employee benefit (that helps retention). Maintaining nonimmigrant status and obtaining immigrant status is of paramount importance to most international employees, often more important than their immediate jobs. It is therefore important that the employee trusts the attorney to look after his or her immigration interests, and understands what is going on in his or her immigration case. The alternative can be suspicion, frustration, and anxiety, none of which is good for employee relations or job performance.

In some cases it may be impractical to have the attorney represent both employer and employee. There may already be a conflict with the employee, there may be confidentiality concerns, or the employer may want the attorney's undivided (i.e., unshared) loyalty. In that case, the attorney must make it clear to the employee that the attorney is representing **only** the employer, advise the employee to get his or her own attorney, and have no contact or direct communication with the employee. In that case, the attorney cannot file with the USCIS any application that the employee signs.

If the attorney does represent both employer and employee, both must agree to this "dual representation" in writing, and both must be informed that there are potential conflicts of interest inherent in the representation. For example, the employer may wish to move the employee to another location, but that could invalidate a labor certification filed on her behalf (delaying her ultimate receipt of the green card). A higher salary may be good for the visa or green card case, but bad for the company's bottom line. An employer may wish to delay the green card case to prevent the employee from leaving the employment. An employer may wish to fire the employee, or the employee may wish to quit. None of these *potential* conflicts of interest prevent dual representation, but if they ever become *actual* conflicts then the attorney usually must stop representing one or both parties.

The obligation of confidentiality also can be a problem if the attorney represents both employer and employee. As the attorney for both employer and employee, it is clear that the lawyer must maintain the confidentiality of all information related to the case with respect to all third parties. However, when both employer and employee are the attorney's clients there can be no secrets with respect to each other, because both are generally entitled to information that may affect the case. To avoid misunderstandings, the attorney must make it clear at the beginning of the case that neither party should confide in the attorney any information that they wish to keep secret from the other client.

In our office, we have three exceptions to the general rule that all information must be shared with both employer and employee. First, we keep secret from the employee all of the employer's information we obtain that is unrelated to and does not appear to impact the case. Second, we keep secret from the employee documents or information that relates to the employer's finances, such as tax returns, financial records and payroll records. Third, if we are given information from the employee about criminal convictions, criminal activity, or health problems, we will not disclose that information to the employer without the employee's consent, even though the information may affect the immigration case. Normally we communicate these policies to both parties at the commencement of the case so that the limits of confidentiality are clear from the beginning.

Judging the competence and diligence of an immigration attorney may be difficult, because the HR manager will not see much of the work of the attorney and his or her staff. However, you can and should examine the work product of the attorney (forms and supporting letters) to make sure that they are persuasive and error-free. Other things you can easily judge are how fast a case is prepared and filed after you give the attorney the assignment, and how fast the attorney responds to your emails and telephone calls. You can judge how quickly and honestly the attorney informs you when problems arise, and whether initial case assessments are realistic or too optimistic. You can judge whether the attorney is honest in the immigration applications. Attorneys are paid to be creative, but presenting the best possible case does not mean subverting the facts or applying for immigration benefits that are not supported in the law or facts. You can be sure that if the attorney is dishonest with the government in the immigration applications, he or she will be dishonest with you.

Other qualities to look for in evaluating your attorney include creativity and optimism. The attorney should be able to consider your unique staffing requirements, and suggest creative solutions that are consistent with the immigration laws (but not so creative that they involve untruthful applications). The attorney should be able to advise you realistically of the strengths and weaknesses of a case, and not just tell you what you want to hear. Armed with that information and the probabilities for success you can make reasonable staffing plans, not only plans for adding workers but also plans for terminating them if their immigration cases do not work out. Finally, your immigration attorney should be your partner in saving costs, including legal fees, where possible.

Conclusion

Immigration laws, and the ways government agencies interpret those laws, are complex and constantly changing. Immigration legal issues can be challenging and it is important to obtain competent legal advice and assistance before hiring foreign workers or applying for their working visas or green cards.

However, there are several reasons why the HR manager should have a working knowledge of the immigration topics summarized in this book. First, the HR manager has an extremely important role in working with the immigration attorney to prepare visa applications, labor certifications, and green card petitions. Second, the HR manager must implement the company's hiring plans to hire foreign workers, and be prepared to hire a foreign worker who is the best applicant for the job. For that, it is helpful to have a working knowledge of the different types of nonimmigrant visas and the eligibility requirements for each. Third, the HR manager must be able to evaluate the immigration attorney, be able to question advice and strategies that may not seem quite right, and perhaps suggest alternatives that the immigration attorney has not proposed. Fourth, the HR manager is responsible for making sure the company does not hire people who are not authorized to work, for properly checking immigration status, and for maintaining proper records such as I-9s and LCA audit files.

Although those responsibilities may at first seem challenging, the reality is that most immigration cases can be handled quickly and efficiently, with a minimal administrative burden and the lowest legal bills your company will ever get. The reward for this extra effort and expense is a competitive workforce, and the ability to expand your hiring pool to include some of the best and the brightest workers in the world.